I0438837

SMILING SUCCESS

YOUR KEY FOR SUCCESS IN

BUSINESS, LOVE, AND LIFE

by
Dr. Steve Thompson
and
Dan Swanson

Smiling Success

by Dr. Steve Thompson and Dan Swanson

Copyright © 2013 by Dr. Steve Thompson and Dan Swanson

www.SmilingSuccess.com • book@SmilingSuccess.com

Smile Time Press

6841 Coit Road • Plano, TX 75024

SmileTimePress.com

First Edition

Ordering Information: Available at www.Amazon.com

Printed in the United States of America

Publisher's Cataloging-in-Publication Data

Thompson, Steve; Swanson, Dan.

Smiling Success: Your Key for Success in Business, Love, and Life

ISBN 978-1-62620-779-0

1. Self help.

2. Health, Mind & Body

3. Business—Motivational. I. Thompson, Steve; Swanson, Dan. II. Title.

Table of Contents

Footnotes

All of the footnotes throughout the book are available in the appendix and to make it easy to click on each reference we've added a clickable version at the following webpage:

www.SmilingSuccess.com/footnotes

Acknowledgement

A special thanks to Tracy Dong for her countless hours
of research and fact finding for this book.

Important Links

1. Smiling Success book website: www.SmilingSuccess.com

2. Two free gifts for you: www.SmilingSuccess.com/2freegifts

3. Dr. Thompson's book: Get Your Smile On: http://www.amazon.com/Get-Your-Smile-Refreshing-Questions/dp/1453866507/ref=tmm_pap_title_0?ie=UTF8&qid=1367313690&sr=1-1

4. Dr. Thompson's dental practice: www.ImagecareDentalGroup.com

5. Dan Swanson's Book: Exit Rich

   - Book website: www.ExitRich.com

   - Amazon book shortcut: www.ExitRich.com/book

   - Amazon book link: http://www.amazon.com/Exit-Rich-Proven-Systematically-Business/dp/1468191322/ref=tmm_pap_title_0?ie=UTF8&qid=1367313774&sr=1-2

Preface

There's just something about a smile. From the wonder of a child's first smile and the excitement of an inviting smile from a new love interest to the intrigue and simplistic beauty of the famous Mona Lisa smile, every human being understands the message of the smile. It enables us to communicate without words, making it one of the greatest forms of unspoken language.

If you picked up this book, you may be facing one or more of the following issues:

- You want to learn how maximize the impact of your smile.

- You are looking to take your business success to the next level.

- You are looking for ways to improve your smile.

- You want to improve how people perceive you in a social or business setting.

- You are finding that your communication ability is lacking, and you are seeking ways to optimize your communication skills to improve your social life or career.

- You are always seeking new ways to make the most of your appearance and think that improving your smile can help you to achieve your goals.

- You have a child or teen who is insecure because of his or her smile, and you want to do all you can to help.

How We Got Started

Before we got started with this book, we did a survey to see how important smiling was to their everyday life.

The results really surprised us and that's what kept us motivated to do the research and finish the book.

Background

We surveyed 109 people. Their average income was $49,000 and their average age was 38; 45% were male and 55% were female.

Findings

Social

- 71% said smiling was either important or very important in their personal relationships
- 83% said smiling was important or very important in their romantic relationships

Sales

- 86% of those involved in sales said a smile helps them land sales

On the Job

- 81% said their smile helped them land a job
- 93% said they would prefer to hire someone who smiles a lot

Shopping

- 44% choose a clerk based on their smile
- 67% said a clerk's unhappy face changed their positive mood to a negative one

- 93% said someone who smiles offers better customer service than those who don't

Dental

- 43% have considered dental options for improving their smile

As you can see from this survey, smiling is important in every part of one's life. And we want to help you maximize your **smiling success**.

What to Expect from this Book

If any of those issues mentioned above line up with where you are right now, it is safe to say that you will find what you need in this book. Below is a quick overview of what you will read in each chapter. Feel free to jump ahead to the section that meets your specific objectives, or go through each chapter to get the most out of the book.

Chapter 1: Why Should You Smile More? – Does your smile really matter? Is it worth the effort? Yes and yes! This chapter outlines the benefits of smiling for your health, family relationships, social life, and career.

Chapter 2: How Smiling Increases Your Business Success – How can optimizing your smile help you to get a new job, promotion or succeed on the job? This chapter goes into more detail about how you can use your smile to achieve career success.

Chapter 3: How Smiling Improves Your Social Life – Struggle to make a great first impression? If so, you may not be making the most of your smile. A healthy, beautiful smile and knowing how to use your eyes and other non-verbal cues can kick your social life up a notch, whether you want to make friends, make a grand entrance at a special event or attract a love interest.

Chapter 4: How Smiling Helps Your Mental Health – A smile can say a lot about your gender, personality and psychological make-up. The way your teeth are displayed in your mouth can determine whether you reveal masculine, feminine, passive or aggressive personality traits. This chapter will show you how dental techniques can finetune the message your smile is sending to the world.

Chapter 5: How Smiling Makes You Healthier – There is great healing power in the smile. This chapter shows how by simply smiling we can prevent negative emotions taking control of our faces, our lives and negatively impacting our health.

Chapter 6: Different Smiles for Different Occasions – Most people are unaware of the many different types of smiles that exist, but this chapter will address smile types and reveal how you can use certain smiles to create the social results you desire—whether that be attracting a new love relationship, relating to family members better, or increasing your chances for success in the workplace.

Chapter 7: What Makes Up a Smile? – There's much more to your smile than teeth. Gums and lips also play an important role, and all parts must work together harmoniously to create a beautiful smile. When each component is optimized, they can effectively work together to help you better communicate with others and send the message you want to send to the people in your life.

Chapter 8: How Smiling Helps Kids and Teens – What does a smile mean to an infant? A child? A teen? How can a smile impact quality of life? This chapter explains the importance of good dental hygiene, smile and dental care modeling, necessary dental procedures as well as how vital unconditional love and nurturing from parents are for children. Children and teens who feel confident in their smiles are better able to handle life's challenges, meet new people and provide a positive impression to those around them, which will benefit them throughout their lives.

Chapter 9: How to Improve Your Smile – Knowledge is power, but it is action that helps you to meet your goals. In this chapter, you will clearly define what your goals are for your smile design, so you can begin to map out your action plan.

Chapter 10: Smiling Success: Putting it all Together – After defining your goals in Chapter 10, you will use this chapter to create your action plan for your best smile possible. After reading a review of each section in the book, you can select which area best pertains to your unique situation and use the action steps at the end of each section to transform your smile and improve your life.

Whether you are ready for extensive dental treatments, or just want to learn what you can do at home to optimize your smile, this book can help. Taking the time to read this book and putting forth the effort to follow through on the action steps will put you on the fast track to achieving the health, wealth, success, and happiness you want for your life.

While you may be groaning at the thought of paying big bucks for expensive dental procedures, you will find that there are ways to improve your smile significantly that won't cost a dime. By learning how to use your eyes, lips and other non-verbal cues with your smile, you can make the most of what God gave you.

Inexpensive over-the-counter treatments can help to improve dental hygiene and the look of your teeth, while just making the effort to smile more can improve your appearance for free. Of course, if you are ready to make your smile a priority, there are ways of supercharging your smile with various dental procedures. Dentists can work with you and your budget to come up with a treatment plan to meet your unique goals and financial constraints.

SmilingSuccess.com: Our Book's Website

Visit the books website and join the list to get free updates, access to the latest resources on the power of smiling in your life. Also go to SmilingSuccess.com/2freegifts to get two free gifts from us as our way of saying thanks.

Where to Go from Here?

You may find it helpful to skip to other chapters that address your unique concerns and situation, but Chapter 2 is really a must-read in order for you to grasp the heart of this book. Gaining an understanding of the benefits of the smile will open your eyes to just how important your smile is to the many different aspects of your life.

Want to land the job of your life? Smiling can help.

Wanting to close more sales? Smiling can help.

Want people to treat you better? Smiling can help.

Struggling in your family relationships? Smiling can help.

Lonely and hoping to attract a new love interest? Smiling can help.

Miserable in your career? Smiling can help.

You will learn exactly how creating your best smile possible will enable you to live life more successfully, experiencing greater joy and fulfillment.

Before you move on to achieving your ideal smile and applying it successfully in your life, you should know that we have included a section in most chapters called smile stories to give you some inspiration from real people who have personally experienced the power of the smile.

Smile Stories... Making a Memorable Impact

About five years ago, a lady stopped me in the cafeteria at work and said 'I remember you from college.' She said 'I can't remember your name, but I know your face, because you always smiled and were so nice to me even though we didn't really know each other.' I was floored because at that time it had been almost 15 years since I'd graduated from college. It was apparent that my routine nature of smiling made a memorable impact on her.

Paula W.

Smile Stories... Autism Smiles

I've always heard a smile is worth a thousand words. This couldn't be truer in the case of my son, Heath, who has autism. We have always said that even through the challenges of autism, he greets each day with a smile on his face. His smile communicates what he often cannot verbalize. We always wonder what is going on in his mind when he struggles to communicate with us verbally. But luckily, at those times his beautiful smile does the talking for him and lets us know what makes him happy. And his smile is so contagious! It's hard not to smile back at someone who smiles at you—especially with Heath, because you see his smile reach his eyes, and you instantly share with him the joy he is feeling inside.

Kim S.

Chapter 1:

Why Should You Smile More?

Smile at each other, smile at your wife,
smile at your husband, smile at your children,
smile at each other – it doesn't matter who it is –
and that will help you grow up in greater love for each other.
Mother Theresa of Calcutta

From the beginning of time, a simple smile has delivered a specific message to others: "I am a friendly person; there's no threat, and you can approach me." The opposite is also true—a frown or scowl sends the message that a person is unhappy, upset, frustrated and unapproachable.

Consider your own life. Who would you most likely want to befriend, converse with, approach or even hire? Someone who is smiling, or someone who has a blank face, no smile, or a frown? The answer is obvious. A smile has more power and influence than any other aspect of a person's disposition, and the advantages of smiling are plentiful.

Smiling offers many benefits to both the person smiling and the recipient of the smile. Of course, we are not talking about a fake smile. A warm, pleasant smile sends the message that you value people and are open to what they have to say.

Perhaps you are not a person who smiles on a regular basis or believe it isn't part of your natural personality and disposition. In light of some fascinating research and statistics, you may find it is worth making the effort to smile.

Consider These Convincing Statistics from Recent Surveys[1]

- 72% of people think of those who smile frequently as being more confident and successful

- 63% of people say that people look best in photos when they are showing their teeth in a smile.

- 99.7% of adults say an attractive smile is an important personal asset.

- 74% of people report that an unattractive smile can hurt a person's chances for business or career success.

- 81% of surveyed individuals indicate that the smile is the most important part of facial appearance.

"Validation" – The Power of a Smile (Kuenne, 2008)[2]

A simple smile has the power to create a change and new perspective in those around us, which in turn builds our own confidence and positive sense of self.

This brief YouTube video entitled "Validation" very clearly illustrates what is possible when you put yourself out there and go for the gold with your smile and a positive perspective.

Real transformation can occur, and this idea is what is at the heart of this book.

View the video and reflect on how much positive change occurred as a result of smiling: http://www.youtube.com/watch?v=Cbk980jV7Ao

---

You can safely assume from this information that something as simple as a smile can actually bring you more success in your career and life. Unlike a new business wardrobe or purchasing a fancy car to boost your confidence and image, **a smile is 100% free**. At no cost and with very little effort you can potentially transform your life and achieve your goals more effectively by turning up the corners of your mouth and baring your pearly whites.

Wait, you may be thinking right now: "My teeth are NOT pearly whites!" It's okay. The best thing you can do is **make the most of what you have**. It is more important to smile than it is to have perfect teeth. If you are truly concerned about the color of your teeth, simply whiten them. It's true that people with whiter, brighter teeth are naturally easier on the eyes. But the real benefit of whitening your teeth is a higher level of confidence, which will lead you to smile more often.

People tend to hesitate to smile or may cover their mouths when they smile, or even show an unnatural smile as a result of their trying to hide teeth that they're not happy with. Even if you are an average-looking Joe or an average-looking Jill and you show an attractive smile, it boosts your overall attractiveness and overall sense of being a confident, successful person. Regardless of your physical appearance or level of a beauty, using an attractive smile with confidence will increase your level of attractiveness to others.

The Benefits of a Consistent Smile

A key to smile success is to be consistent in your smiling behavior. Show your smile often and it will influence how others see you and relate to you on a daily basis. It will transform people's impression of you, which in turn benefits all relationships and interactions in your life—whether those interactions are with friends, family, co-workers, or potential love interests.

Many people are unaware of what is going on with their facial expressions as they make their way through the day. Yet those around us are continually aware of the messages we send with our faces. Children are especially in-tune to facial expressions. A three-year old may see her mother frowning and ask, "Are you angry?" even if the lack of smiling was not a result of anger, but rather stress or another personal issue, or even focused concentration on a task. Still, the child is able to pick up on the negative energy from the frown and it causes concern for her.

Likewise, many people go through their days with expressions on their faces that are negative, and they are completely unaware of the impressions they are giving to others and how people perceive them as a result of their facial expressions. If you have a smile or a grin or a pleasant look on your face, you're going to be more approachable and more attractive. People are going to see you in a positive light versus somebody who is scowling or frowning or displaying another negative expression.

Ted Presents

In a Ted.com presentation entitled "The Hidden Power of Smiling,"[3] HealthTap CEO Ron Gutman points to a variety of studies that reveal the power of smiling. He addresses British research that found smiling generates the same level of brain stimulation as up to 2,000 bars of chocolate. According to Gutman, the same study found that smiling is as stimulating as receiving up to 16,000 pounds of Sterling in cash. However, it is the consistent smiling that enables the individual to reap these brain-stimulating rewards. One smile may not make a significant impact, but repeated smiling will positively impact the person who is smiling as well as those who encounter the smile.

You may wonder how a smile can benefit you in your personal and professional life. Take a look at this graphic illustrating how a smile can start a cycle of positivity for you and those around you:

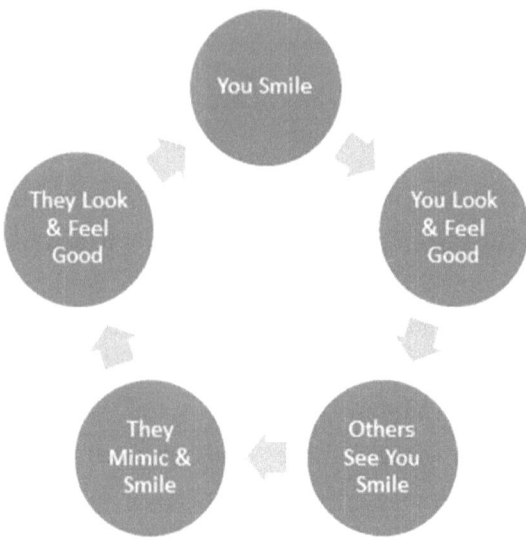

From Ted.com "The Hidden Power of Smiling" with Ron Gutman[4]

Smiling throughout the day will enhance your mood and can potentially change your view of the world, because the smile is likely to come back to you. Smiles are universal. They convey a sense of warmth and invoke positive feelings among all people, all ethnicities, from a variety of backgrounds and life experiences.

A consistent smile is enhanced with eye contact—looking into someone's eyes as you smile, talk or listen to the person. Of course, you want to avoid "staring" in an uncomfortable way. Keep a pleasant facial expression that gives the impression you value the person and what he or she has to say. Focus on what the person is saying and avoid looking in other directions or appearing distracted, which tends to turn people off.

This eye contact-smile combination carries with it significant power to positively impact those around you. It's been said the eyes are the window into the soul, but more accurately it is the eyes and smile that reveal the window into an individual's personality.

In addition to the general benefits of smiling, there is a plethora of anecdotal and research evidence regarding the benefits of smiling in specific areas of your life, including:

- Health
- Relationships with Family
- Relationships with Friends & Potential Love Interests
- Career and Work Place Success

How Smiling Benefits Your Health

Dr. Mark Stibich, a behavioral change expert, shared in his article entitled "Top 10 Reasons to Smile"[5] that research has shown smiling can significantly improve your health in a variety of ways. In his writings, Dr. Stibich points to five health-related benefits of smiling:

1. **Stress Relief**

Stress can really show up in our faces. Smiling helps to prevent us from looking tired, worn down, and overwhelmed. When you are stressed, take time to put on a smile. The stress should be reduced and you'll be better able to take action.

Smiling may help to reduce symptoms associated with anxiety. Stibich said, "If you can slow your breathing down and change your expression, you may be able to turn around the stress cascade. Chronic stress can lead to damage to the body and mind. Reducing stress in turn may lower blood pressure, improved digestion, regulated blood sugar and potential neurotic episodes brought on by long-term anxiety.

2.   Strengthening the Immune System

Smiling helps the immune system to work better. When you smile, immune function improves possibly because you are more relaxed. Prevent the flu and colds by smiling.

3.   Decreasing Blood Pressure

When you smile, there is a measurable reduction in your blood pressure. Give it a try if you have a blood pressure monitor at home. Sit for a few minutes, take a reading. Then smile for a minute and take another reading while still smiling. Do you notice a difference?

4.   Releasing Endorphins, Natural Pain Killers and Serotonin

Studies have shown that smiling releases endorphins, natural pain killers, and serotonin in the brain. Together these three make us feel good. Smiling is a natural drug. Smiling can lift your spirits. A study conducted by the British Dental Health Foundation showed the act of smiling to dramatically improve one's mood.

5.   Lifting the Face and Making Us Look Younger

The muscles we use to smile lift the face, making a person appear younger. Don't go for a face lift, just try smiling your way through the day – you'll look younger and feel better.

Even over one hundred years ago, scientists were onto the health benefits of the smile. *Smile! The Secret Science of Smiling* shares this century-old research: In 1907, a Russian immigrant to France named Israel Weinbaum wrote that "facial gestures in general have regulatory and restorative functions for the vascular systems of the head".[6]

According to Star (2009), Dr. Robert Zajonc, once a clinical researcher and psychologist from the University of Michigan confirmed that Weinbaum was correct.

Zajonc explained that emotional experiences result (positive or negative) in change in the blood flow and vascular system. Smiling has the effect of "cooling off our brains," according to Zajonc. It causes vascular dilation and increases the blood flow, which in turn keeps the brain cool, as the brain functions optimally within a narrow temperature range.

Zajonc goes onto explain that the brain cannot tolerate temperature variations as well as other organs, so we require smiling to keep the temperature where it needs to be in order to keep us feeling well. Furthermore, the structure of the mouth and eyes as we smile promotes that good feeling by regulating brain temperature, meaning that smiling—even in a room by ourselves—can promote good health!

We'll cover in more detail the benefits smiling has in regards to physical health in Chapter 5.

How Smiling Benefits Relationships with Family Members

When it comes to family members, children and adults alike respond positively to smiling. A family member who wakes up to our smile has a better start to their day. On the flip side, waking up to a frown or blank face, can lead to a negative beginning and a feeling of discouragement or frustration.

Consider your own personal experience with this. Think back to when you were a child. Do you recall moments when your parents were smiling at you and other moments when they were not smiling at you? If you can recall those moments, chances are you can bring back the feelings you had during those times. Receiving a smile from someone brings forth a positive emotional response. Even parents who must discipline or redirect their children, can smile in a loving way to show them they care and maintain love even during necessary disciplinary times.

It comes back to the power of smiling consistently. It's a way of showing unconditional love to family members that they so desperately need. This need does not go away as adults. Your spouse, significant other, parents, or adult siblings have a deep need for this love and acceptance as much as your children. By smiling, even during difficult or frustrating life experiences or disagreements, you are illustrating your unconditional love for those around you. There is great power in this type of emotional display.

It makes sense that parents who smile often during a child's infancy and young developmental years tend to have children who report low levels of stress in contrast to children whose parents did not smile often. Furthermore, children learn best from parent-modeling. Parents who demonstrate positive emotions to children will find that their children mirror what they see. Smile now, so your children will smile. It sounds simple and almost trivial, but the implications for this basic behavior change are astounding.

As children experience the difficulties and stresses of the adolescent and teenage years, they may be more likely to come to a parent for advice and comfort if the parent is a "smiler." Parents who smile seem more approachable and accepting—two important factors that children require to feel safe.

Would you like to ensure your children have lower stress levels as they walk through life into adulthood? Smiling at them often is a simple way to help your children grow up to be well-adjusted adults who pass on that smile to others.

Children Instinctively Know the Power of Smiling

Children learn early the power of a smile. Have you ever approached one of your children or a child you that know to admonish them for poor behavior, only to find them smiling at you sweetly? Your anger can dissolve in a second when you receive a loving smile from a child. While you may need to continue to disciple or correct for the behavior, it is nearly impossible for most people to continue to be filled with anger. The smile disarms anger and creates warmth and love in its place.

Studies have revealed that children smile as many as 400 times per day. Smiling is instinctive for most children[7]. They can be crying one moment, and smiling brightly the next. What causes this consistent smile to go away as we age? As adults we tend to forget smiling is a tool that is ours to use—for free. Perhaps adults become jaded, or too wrapped up in the stressors of day-to-day life. But getting back in touch with this child-like tool can have very positive implications for us when it comes to relating to family members, as well as other people in our lives.

How Smiling Benefits Relationships with Friends & Potential Love Interests

Relationship struggles is a primary cause for heartache and stress in many people I encounter. They feel alone or abandoned. They want to share their lives with someone special, but can't seem to make a connection with someone. They feel like everyone else is finding a spouse, while they are still on square one. Or perhaps they have friends, but are continually experiencing drama or can't seem to express themselves in a way that creates positive interactions with others.

While I can't say a smile is the answer to all of these issues, a smile is a tool that is significantly under-used in today's society, and can truly make a powerful difference in your experiences with friends and potential love interests.

When you smile, it transmits a message to others. Messages like:

- Hey, I'm glad you are here.

- Nice to see you.

- I care about you.

- I think you are significant.

- I value you and what you have to say.

All of these things are communicated with a smile. So it is safe to say when you walk through life without a smile, you are missing out on communicating this effectively to others—even if you feel these things in your heart. You may value the other person, be happy to see them and have interest in what they have to say, but if you frown or have a blank look upon your face, they will not receive these messages from you.

You know how it is difficult to express emotion through e-mail or online interactions when people cannot physically hear your tone of voice? It's much like this when you try to communicate to others without a smile. Words are taken the wrong way. Tones of speech are misunderstood. Even if you are communicating a positive message, without a smile, the message can fall flat or go unheard.

Philip's Problem

Consider this story from an article called "Smile"[8] sharing a common experience people who struggle to smile may have:

Philip has a very big problem. Whenever he enters a room, everyone ignores him. Every time he gets on the bus to go to school, the bus driver simply nods and looks away. Most of Philip's peers almost never have conversations with him, and the impression around school is that he is a grump who gets mad at just about anything. Even his teachers are edgy with him, and tell him that he has a "chip on his shoulder." "Why does this always happen to me?" Philip asks himself. "Why does everyone treat me this way?" Unaware that he is the source of the problem, Philip is unable to understand why others view him in an unpleasant manner. While he always has a lot to say, Philip's communication skills are lacking because he never learned to use one of the most powerful methods of communicating thoughts, moods, feelings and emotions. Philip simply never smiles!

Often people who struggle to build strong relationships with friends or love interests have an underlying issue in that they do not smile regularly. It can be a major roadblock to positive relationships and one of which the offender is completely unaware.

If you are unsure as to whether your lack of smiling is impeding your ability to connect with others, it may be time to ask people around you what they think. It may seem awkward at first, but it can truly help you to gain an understanding of how you appear to those around you.

Ask a parent, teacher or friend if they consider you a person who smiles often. Chances are, you can learn a lot about the perception others may have of you just by asking this simple question. Remember to consider whatever they have to say as constructive criticism. You can take their honest feedback and use it to improve yourself as you move forward in this process.

A Smile: The Primary Factor in Attaining Eye-Appeal[9]

Women in beauty pageants are often obsessed with having physical beauty. This interesting video below shows how smiling is perhaps the most important aspect of a lovely appearance. It illustrates how while it is impossible and unnatural to smile continuously, you can maintain a pleasant look on your face while smiling with your eyes.

In Venezuela, the smile is so important to beauty pageant contestants, that many have special crown-lengthening procedures done in order to improve their smiles., We believe this shows how essential a nice smile is to your level of attractiveness. Watch the video here: http://www.youtube.com/watch?v=ok7p2k6jo28 or search how to win beauty pageants

---

Why You Seem More Attractive with a Smile

Everyone has had an attractive person—a beautiful girl or a handsome guy, catch their eye. If you stop to think about it, you will likely discover one of the first things you notice about the attractive person is their smile. If the person is not smiling, you are likely not quite as interested. They don't seem to have that magnetism that makes you want to learn more about them.

If the person has a nice consistent smile, it really gets your attention. It makes them seem more beautiful than they are. A mildly attractive young man can appear much more handsome when he has a smile on his face. He seems more approachable and desirable. The magnetism is there, because the smile is present.

Of course, there are situations in which teeth must be corrected or whitened in order to create a smile that gives the desired impact. Discolored or crooked teeth cannot be made right by smiling. So if that is an issue for you, by all means do what you can to make the most of the teeth you have.

But outside of this issue, smiling is the singular most impactful thing you can do to improve your appearance. The act of smiling will bring you more confidence, and will increase the positive response you receive from others. As they smile back at you, your confidence builds even more. It's a powerful cycle that only you can put into motion.

Let's take a look at some beginner tips to help you to become more self-aware when it comes to your smile:

- Be aware of your facial expressions. Many people do not realize how much time they spend frowning or scowling. As mentioned above, ask others who know you well to evaluate your facial expressions, or just take some time each day to focus on self-awareness to assess how often you frown, scowl and how often you smile.

- If you do not feel confident in your appearance, keep at the forefront of your mind that your smile is the first thing people will notice about you—not the size of your biceps, nose or thighs, not the color of your hair, but your smile! Keep that in mind and then smile the next time you meet someone new for the first time—and put the other concerns out of your mind.

- You can smile at people whom you know and people you want to attract, but also to others whom you may not like as much. With a smile, we offer goodwill to another person; it has the power to smooth over negative feelings and alleviate tense situations. People unconsciously respond in a positive way to a smile. Your smile may set off a chain-reaction in which a former friend sees you in a different way, responds to you positively and you start a new friendship.

The Smile Experiment

Here's an opportunity to conduct a little self-assessment that can be very eye-opening and enlightening when it comes to the impact your smile can have on others and yourself. For this experiment, take the following steps:

- Go for a walk for approximately one hour in a public place where you will encounter many people. The grocery store, shopping mall, or a popular walking trail are good places.

- When you begin your walk, smile at each and every person you encounter. Focus on giving a genuine smile, which may be challenging. Just do your best.

- Notice how many people respond to your smile and the way in which they respond to you.

- The next day, go on another walk in the same place and do not smile at anyone.

- Notice how many people smiled this time.

After the experiment, take some time to reflect on the types of responses you received on the two different walks. How did the responses differ? How did you feel at the end of each walk? Chances are, you felt much more positive after the first

walk in which you focused on smiling, because many people…
(not all, but many) smiled back at you. That kind of positivity
is contagious.

Can you recognize how your interactions with others
might be impacted if you make an effort to smile consistently?

If smiling makes you more attractive to all people, it's absolutely
true that the act makes you more attractive to those of the opposite sex.
Single people who are using one of the many popular dating websites
should take this into consideration as they upload their profile
pictures. A profile picture in which you are smiling will make a much
stronger impact than any other expression. We'll cover this topic more
in Chapter 4 where we will provide coaching for smiling properly in
a profile picture. But whether you are posting a picture of yourself, or
meeting someone for the first time, a smile and direct eye contact are
the two most important things you should be "wearing" if your goal is
to appear attractive to the other person.

In *How to Win Friends and Influence People*,[10] Dale Carnegie
shares a powerful statement about the power of a smile in relationships:

*It costs nothing, but creates much. It enriches those who receive,
without taking away from those who give. It happens in a flash
and the memory of it sometimes lasts forever. It creates happiness
in the home, fosters good will in a business, and is the countersign
of friends. It is rest to the weary, daylight to the discouraged,
sunshine to the sad, and nature's best antidote for trouble. Yet it
cannot be bought, begged, borrowed, or stole, for it is something
that is no earthly good to anybody till it is given away…*

How Smiling Benefits Career & Workplace Success

As we've discussed, a smile makes you much more attractive to others, makes you more approachable and helps you to build relationships with others. Another important way your smile can benefit your life is in your career. A smile makes you more likeable, confident, social, and, thus, more hirable.

Your smile can be a great asset if you are seeking employment or working toward a raise or promotion. Employers want to hire employees who can do the job well, but part of almost any job is working well with others and being a generally pleasant person. That's where your smile comes in. Your smile gives the impression that you can work well with others and that you will be a friendly employee to represent the company.

Dr. Charles Martin, DDS, founder of the Richmond Smile Center is quoted as saying, "Essentially, all things being equal, if two people have equal capabilities, **the one who smiles more is going to get the job**."[11] It couldn't be stated any more clearly: **Your smile is something you can and should leverage in your career**.

Some people have the mistaken impression that a smile can make them seem less serious or even appear silly. However, all of the anecdotal evidence and research points to a smile being a positive when it comes to your career potential and success.

Just a few of the ways smiling can benefit your career and your workplace, whether you're an employee, a manager, an executive or a business owner:

- Build rapport with customers
- Give value-added services to customers
- Create loyal customers

- People want to work with you

- People say good things about you

- Managers appreciate your attitude and give good reviews

A Today.com article entitled "Hey, Good Lookin', Your Job Outlook Lookin' Good"[12] claims that beautiful people are seen as more valuable employees and harder workers. Since we have already covered that smiling makes you attractive, it is safe to deduct that a consistent, genuine smile can mean a higher salary for you. That's a pretty high return on investment, considering your smile is free!

Smiles Help Diffuse Workplace Tension and Promote Better Team Work

The workplace can be an unpleasant place for many. With stress levels and tensions high, a smile can be your secret weapon to bringing some light into a challenging environment. You can instantly elevate the mood of your co-workers, or even your boss, when you shine a smile. It's a way to bring everyone back to reality and away from the hostility of a tense environment. It can bring the focus away from the stress and back to the solutions to remedy the situation.

Of course, there are certain very serious situations in that a smile would be inappropriate and could be viewed as offensive rather than "light," so it is important to use good judgment in these types of scenarios.

From preventing arguments to brightening a co-workers bad day at the office, your smile can help you to be viewed as a positive peacemaker who is a great asset to the company. Let's face it, most people walk around the office stressed out, frustrated, and not enjoying their day, but when you put forth the effort to smile, you can bring a moment of happiness to another person's day and simultaneously improve your own mood and outlook.

An Industrial Organization Psychology textbook[13] explains that an employer can ask an employee to stay late to work on a report, and if she says it with a smile, the employee is much more likely to stay to complete the report. In this way it seems more like a pleasant request, but when the same question is asked without a smile, it seems more like a demand that is not as often met with goodwill.

This same text book addresses tension between co-workers and explains how a smile "kills them with kindness" and can get you out of gossip situations, or other less-than-professional conversations in which you do not want to be involved. A smile gives you the power to influence others—whether it is promoting the right way to behave at work, or convincing someone to see things from your perspective.

How a CEO Can Reduce Office Stress: Put on a Smile

Studies have shown that the social environment is the No. 6 contributor to workforce burnout, says Scott.[14] The CEO may think that his or her demeanor doesn't directly affect staff, but it's been shown that workers read the mood of the boss for clues about performance or job security. CEOs can calm those fears by being more open with employees – often that means simply smiling more often, talking with employees about family or hobbies, or having a laugh and cracking jokes. In turn, these simple steps will boost morale, bring people closer, and perhaps even warding off burnout, says Scott.

However, it's important not to emulate Steve Carell's character on *The Office*. Avoid jokes about co-worker's accents, hygiene, and workplace behavior. Too often workplace jokes border on offensive and can actually induce stress, found a recent study by Christopher

LeGrow, a psychology professor at Marshall University, which is based in Huntington, West Virginia. The study reported that around 70 percent of workplace jokes made fun of co-workers' age, sexual orientation, and weight. Forty percent of those polled admitted that they themselves had made fun of a co-worker. "Stick with light-hearted, fun jokes," Scott advises.

Smile Stories... Mean People, Beware of My Killer Smile!!

It was during my freshman year, during hazing week, of all times, that I realized what my mother was trying to say. We will always have to deal with not-so-nice people every once in a while; that's just life. Some of them will be darned right mean and nasty for reasons you will never understand. The trick is to take away their power. And the best way to do that is to smile. Smile at them every chance you get. Smile at them when they are calling you names. Smile at them in the hall. Smile at them in gym class. You can never smile too much!! Mean people cannot defend themselves against random, unexplainable kindness.

Political candidates understand the influential power of smiling well. They flash their largest smile to voters for a reason—it makes them look good, approachable, friendly, trustworthy, and they want to earn your vote.

In addition to influencing others and promoting good relationships with co-workers and employers, a smile can help you to keep cool under pressure when things get tense at work. By smiling in high-pressure work situations, it will have a calming effect on yourself and those around you—illustrating that you have it "together" and can do your job well in any situation.

Smile: Make an Impact in All Areas of Your Life

This chapter makes just a dent in the details regarding how you can make a positive impact in all areas of your life with a genuine, consistent smile. In the following chapters, we'll provide more how-to information to help you discover your own personal best smile and how you can use it to build your confidence, improve your health, increase attractiveness, and develop healthier relationships with those around you.

Action Items

Part 1: Ask 10 people you regularly interact with:

- If you smile a lot
- If they consider you a happy person
- (Note – don't argue with them)

Part 2: Spend the next 7 days intentionally smiling as much as you can

- Did the world treat you back better or worse?
- How did it make you feel?

Part 3: Ask the same 10 people as in Part 1:

- Did they notice you smiling more?
- Do they now consider you a happier person than the last time you asked them

Next

Now that we've seen the overall benefits of smiling, let's see what smiling does for you in business.

Allison's Personal Story

Tell us a little about yourself

I started my professional modeling and acting journey about nine years ago.

At that time I was self-conscious of my smile. I had an overbite since I could remember. And when I was 14, I was told I needed braces and jaw surgery but my mom, for whatever reason, decided not to go that course because she didn't want to see me go through the surgery and everything associated with it, so I never got it taken care of.

So when I was in my mid to late 20s, I got my first agent and I had mentioned to him at the time that I was a little bit self-conscious of my smile. And he said something to the effect that, well, yeah, it would be better if you had a nicer smile, but there are other roles that you can play where you don't have to have perfect teeth.

My smile kept bothering me for the next couple of years. I would go out on auditions, but I wasn't really booking a lot of stuff.

So what did you decide to do?

I finally decided when I was 30 to go and get a consultation and see what it would require to get my teeth fixed and my jaw aligned. I needed corrective surgery.

And I had to have my teeth aligned before they could even do the surgery.

So I got my braces. I wore them for three years prior to surgery.

It was major surgery.

I was finally able to get my braces off about six months after the surgery and then I was like so happy. I mean I have never regretted it for a day.

Sounds like you were really happy with the results.

As a matter of fact, it was probably one of the best decisions I've ever made in my life. Whenever I started auditioning after that, that's when I started booking work. And now I see that every time my agent sends me some kind of casting notice, just about every time for anything, for modeling, for commercials, a nice smile is so, so important to those.

And I know that that's one of the things that helps me stand out from the competition. On a lot of audition notices it'll say, "Must have nice smile" or it always says something about a smile so I know that my agent is sending me out on these things because she knows that I fit into that category.

I've told my husband that the years I spent in braces and the surgery, it's paid for itself just in the bookings that I've gotten since then.

Was there anything else you needed to have a great smile?

We pick up tips and tricks from photographers. One of the things that they tell you to do is when you are smiling, the way to make it look natural is to pretend like you're saying hello to a child in the camera with your eyes. It's just one of those tricks that helps you to look more natural when you're smiling.

I'm asked to do all kinds of smiles, big smiles or smaller smiles. Whenever we're on modeling shoots, the photographer usually gives direction about different ways, different looks and they give you different scenarios so I have to use my acting background in the modeling to kind of create the look that they want for the pictures.

They want your whole face to light up when you smile. It's not just about what's going on from here down. You have to be feeling it.

You have to look at the camera and pretend like you're seeing somebody. That's in acting, too, not just in modeling. But you've really got to see a person in the camera that you're talking to, somebody that you can connect with. And when you can see that, then it makes your smile natural, like you would smile at a person in real life.

When you walk into a room for an audition, the first thing you want to do is make eye contact and smile if the client is in the room. You want to put people at ease and make them feel comfortable.

And when you smile, I think it naturally causes you to relax and you feel more confident and you feel happier and more outgoing. So I think the body language actually just kind of comes along with the smile if you're genuinely happy to be there and you just feel so much more relaxed and confident.

Any advice for others?

It's important to accept yourself the way you are. But if there's something that's consistently been bothering you that's easily fixed, then I absolutely say go for it. I mean there's no reason to not do it.

Even looking back, yeah, it was several years in my life in braces. It was a rough recovery from the surgery. But I don't regret it for a minute. As a matter of fact, I think it was one of the best decisions I've ever made. So if there's something that you can do to feel better, then by all means, go for it.

Chapter 2:

How Smiling Increases Your Business Success

This seems very simple, but it's amazing how people's moods and words are misjudged because their expressions are often overly-serious. A smile shows that you like yourself; you like your current place in the world and you're happy with the people you're interacting with. No one will say you're crabby if you're smiling. A smile says I'm approachable and confident.
Mercedes Alfaro, President, First Impression Management
www.firstimpressionmanagement.com

It's no secret that your body language impacts your success in business, but it isn't as well known that a smile is one of the most influential aspects of one's body language. The success of any meeting, conversation, or encounter with another person in business begins the moment the other person focuses their eyes on you—and the type of expression you have upon your face in that moment determines the first impression you make. The other person lays eyes upon you and in one brief moment makes a judgment call on who you are and what you are all about.

The smile or lack of smile is one of the first things another person will notice when they are developing their initial impression. A simple act of smiling creates a welcoming, friendly aura that words simply cannot create on their own. Smiling conveys interest, empathy, positivity, and confidence. Are these the characteristics that you would like to portray in the workplace?

Let's Put the Question Another Way

Are these characteristics (interest, empathy and positivity) you would like to see in your co-workers and/or employees?

Sometimes it isn't always easy to see the importance of our own smiles, but when we stop and consider the type of appearance and image we find most appealing to us in the workplace, we begin to understand the power of the smile in business.

Image is very important to business success, so it is important to consider how others see you and to understand what small changes you can put into action to make the most of your business persona. Making an effort to smile may be the act that can push you to the top of a list of interview candidates, help you to close the big sale, or help you become an effective manager or CEO.

However, a smile that is unnatural, forced or too strong can put forth a less-than-genuine vibe, so it is important to understand the right timing and approach for your smile in business situations. We recommend first to establish your presence in a room and then flash a confident smile to gain and increase respect.

How to Use a Smile in Job Interviews

While some may like to believe that qualifications matter more than appearance when it comes to getting a new job or a promotion, the truth is that in our society appearance matters…a lot! As we covered previously, people who are viewed as attractive are more likely to be successful in their careers, and this is a great argument for making the most of your personal appearance as you prepare for job interviews.

Your smile is a focal point during a first impression, so it makes sense that you should do all you can to enhance your smile. You need not have perfect teeth, but it is important to take care of what you have. Over-the-counter teeth whiteners and whitening toothpastes are easy to access and provide a simple way for you to give your smile a boost for important business meetings, such as a job interview.

In situations where someone has severe problems with their teeth, it may be a good idea to have dental work done to avoid making a less-than-professional impression.

Outside of the appearance of your smile, it can be a challenge for some to actually remember to do it at all. As you prepare for a job interview, you will want to spend time practicing your smile and planning to use it during your interview. Not only will the smile provide an impression that you are enthusiastic and confident, it will also relax you. A smile is proven to alleviate tension you may carry in your shoulder and neck area.

Try it now: Smile! Do you feel your muscles relax? This can definitely come in handy during interviews, as you want to create a confident, relaxed image.

Is Your Smile Really THAT Important to Your Career?[15]

Previous consumer studies have proved that a beautiful smile will make you more attractive. But according to research conducted by Beall Research & Training of Chicago, a new smile will make you appear more intelligent, interesting, successful and wealthy to others as well. Dr. Anne Beall, a social

---

psychologist and market research professional carried out the independent study on behalf of the American Academy of Cosmetic Dentistry (AACD). In 2004, her study revealed that **74% of adults feel an unattractive smile can hurt a person's chances for career success.**

When asked, *"What is the first thing you notice in a person's smile?"* The most common responses were:

- Straightness
- Whiteness & Color of Teeth
- Cleanliness of Teeth
- Sincerity of Smile
- Any Missing Teeth?
- Sparkle of Smile

And when asked, "What types of things do you consider make a smile unattractive?" The most common responses were:

- Discolored, Yellow, or Stained Teeth
- Missing Teeth
- Crooked Teeth
- Decaying Teeth & Cavities
- Gaps & Spaces in Teeth
- Dirty Teeth

And finally, when respondents were asked, "What would you most like to improve about your smile?" The most common response was:

- Whiter & Brighter Teeth

The Consequences of Not Smiling in a Job Interview

I've hired quite a few people over the years and perhaps I'm a little biased since I work in the smile industry, but it's always very interesting that when somebody comes in to interview, one of the first things that I notice about them is their smile.

We're trying to project a professional image in our practice to our patients, and I would be reluctant to hire somebody who didn't have a great smile or people that maybe have a good smile but don't use it.

I've had employees in the past who had a tendency to be a little bit grouchy, who didn't smile, and it just didn't work well with what we're trying to accomplish in our business.

Likewise, I've seen people who have come into our office for an interview, and I could tell that they weren't confident about themselves or about their smile because they were not smiling. They looked down a lot; they didn't make eye contact.

Sometimes I chalk that up to being a little bit nervous, but my philosophy is during the interview process, if somebody doesn't have the self-confidence to smile, to look you in the eye during that time, I can't expect them to ever show me any different type of behavior, even if I were to hire them.

It's safe to say that most people try to put their best foot forward during an interview, and if you have a great personality, even if you're nervous, we're still going to see that personality during the interview. And so, no smile, no eye contact, no personality during that initial interview is just a huge red flag.

Obviously those types of interviews are over pretty quick if I'm involved or my hiring manager is involved. A great smile, even a not-so-great smile, and using it sets you miles apart from your competition during the job interview process.

3 Job Interview Tips to Stand Out and Get Hired

1. Smile

You want to make a memorable impression on each person with whom you come in contact during your interview and visit to the business location. By smiling, making eye contact, shaking hands and speaking the name of each person you meet, you will stand out among the pack of candidates. The very simple actions can go a long way toward displaying your confidence and friendliness—which are essential attributes of a good hire.

When you smile, use a genuine, teeth-baring smile. Show that you are happy to be there and that you are positive about this interview process and potential job. Keep smiling throughout the interview.

The different kinds of smiles may be necessary throughout the interview. (See more about this in Chapter 9).

2. Make Eye Contact

Making eye contact is good, but holding eye contact throughout the interview process is extremely important. It shows you have nothing to hide and are fully-engaged in the interview. Each time you start eye contact, hold until the other person breaks it off.

3. Shake Hands and Say Their Name

Use a firm handshake to display your confidence, and then speak each person's name clearly to show your attention to detail and people skills.

The better you look, the more you can earn.

It's no secret that when your smile is radiant, when your teeth are straight and white, when your facial appearance is attractive, you can create a welcoming first impression. The "million-dollar smile" could be taken literally for executives—in how much they earn because of it.

Recent research shows a connection between how much is in your paycheck and your appearance. A study released by the Federal Reserve Bank of St. Louis found that more attractive people earned 5% more an hour than their less good-looking counterparts (CNN/Money, 2005).

These tips may seem obvious, but it is amazing how many interviewees neglect these areas. It is easy to get so wrapped up in what you plan to say with your words that you forget the impact your body language makes.

Selling Yourself with a Smile (In the Interview and Beyond)[16]

Smiling in a job interview is a good way to make a positive first impression, but it is also a good way to promote a confident, professional image once you've landed the job. Whether you are hoping for a promotion, or just want to reach the highest level of success possible in your career, smiling attracts people to you and shows others you are a likable person—someone they want to hire and work with.

Consider the people whom you enjoy working with the most. Chances are, they are friendly, out-going and have a contagious, inviting smile. Someone who is positive and upbeat with a smile creates that kind of aura wherever they go. That is exactly the kind of person other people want to work with in a business environment, which is why you want to become THAT person.

In addition to your influence on your employer and co-workers, smiling can have a big impact on your success with customers and prospects. Again, consider where you like to shop. It's likely that you would choose a business where the staff members are smiling and friendly over a business where the employees did not smile.

This is really a no-brainer, yet far too many businesses seem to have employees working with customers who can barely crack a smile or make eye contact. A grunt is the best they can do. Smiling takes such little effort, yet can reap big rewards when it comes to building rapport with customers and creating customer loyalty.

Different Types of Smiles[17]

A study conducted by scientists at the University of Portsmouth identified different types of smiles and revealed that listeners can identify the type of smile based on sound alone (Science Daily, Jan. 16, 2008).

Researchers identified 50 different types of smiles, including:

- Open Smile—truest and most intense with lips drawn back, cheeks raised and crows-feet wrinkles showing.

- Suppressed Smile—person tries to hide the smile by pulling lips in or down.

Listeners could identify which of the numerous smile types the speaker had even when they could not see the speaker.

Speakers with "smilier" voices tend to be better received by their audiences.

> Using the most genuine smile possible when you talk (whether you are seen or not) may be one of the best ways to win-over your audience.

If a customer or client approaches you with questions about products or services, you want them to feel comfortable and at ease and respond in a way that makes them glad they asked you. This is what good sales technique is all about.

Service with a smile is the number one method for getting and keeping customers. In fact, in the typical training for a salesperson, the trainees are taught to master the art of smiling.

The Importance of a Smile in Customer Service

Smiling makes you a more attractive hire, a more productive salesperson, but it can also provide added value to your customer service efforts. In J. Blount's *People Buy You: The Real Secret to What Matters Most in Business*[18] the author explains that a customer buys the customer service as well as the product during the sale. She illustrates how good customer service with a smile will keep the customer thinking about you, not just the product, and it is this behavior that will bring the customer back for repeat purchases.

However, if the customer service is lacking and it is unfriendly, the customer can easily be persuaded to purchase from another business with better customer service practices. Blount uses the phrase "always leave them wanting more." While it applies to performers and artists, it also applies to customer service.

When you share a smile with customers and show them you care about their customer satisfaction, this will leave a positive impact that will have them wanting more of what you have to offer.

A Tidd & Lockard study from way back in 1978 showed how influential a smile is on customer satisfaction. It revealed that the strength of an employee's smile predicts the customer satisfaction and is even more influential that eye contact or verbal greetings. This same study found that an employee's overall smile strength directly impacts the customer's overall smile strength and service quality ratings during the encounter.[19]

> *...the strength of an employee's smile predicts the customer satisfaction and is even more influential that eye contact or verbal greetings.*

It's fascinating once we can begin to understand just how much power there is in the smile when it comes to creating positive business interactions on a variety of different levels. But this study shows us it's not just any smile, but a strong, genuine smile that makes "customers appraise an employee as more friendly competent, and thus the encounter as more satisfying."

Ultimately, this study that still proves useful today recommends the following:

> *Managers need to hire employees who are more likely to be genuinely positive and to foster a workplace that enhances authentic positive moods and expressions. ...It is important to make sure that hiring and training focus on the quality of service encounters overall (e.g. friendliness, efficiency, accuracy) rather than simply on putting the customer in a good mood.*

Smiling during a customer encounter has an interesting effect on how the customer feels after that interaction. The post-encounter mood of a customer predicted how satisfied they were going to be with that business and their likelihood to come back, visit again, and to have positive thoughts about that business. It's important that your customers come away with a positive feeling and a smile, because if they do they're more likely to come and visit you again.

The truth is, people buy from whom they like, know, and trust. And they'll like you more, they'll trust you more, and get to know you more, the more confidence you have with your smile and if you're not feeling confident enough to smile in a sales situation, they're not going to trust you.

It is for this reason it is important to grasp the perspective that customers are going to buy **you.** Your product actually ends up being peripheral.

The Smile and the First Impression

It's been said many times: you only get one chance to make a good first impression. Some very smart companies have their highest-paid folks answering the phone for this very reason—giving a powerful, positive first impression. I've talked to many receptionists who are making $70,000 plus because the companies want to put their very best face forward for each new call.

No matter whether it's in person or on the phone, you may not get a chance for a second encounter. However, by ensuring you have a skilled, friendly, person who knows how to smile with his or her face and voice greeting customers, you are doing everything you can to make the most of the first impression.

Customer Service Tip: Smile through the Phone

A smile in customer service is important even when the customer cannot see your face. Customer service experts suggest that customers can sense the employee's smile through the phone by picking up on non-verbal messages, such as:

- Accents

- Emphasis on words

- Pauses

- Volume of speech

If the message is delivered with a smile, these non-verbal cues will come through with positivity and sincerity. But without a smile, the exact same words can seem negative.

When there is no smile or facial expression to see with their eyes, customers listen even more closely to "hear" the smile in the voice and language. Simply making an effort to smile while on the phone can increase the customer's satisfaction with the phone customer service experience.

Many customer service businesses put a mirror next to each station so agents can notice if they are smiling or not.

It is of critical importance to ensure a prospect's first interaction with your business is a positive one. When the first interaction is a phone call, the goal is to make the prospect feel like the person on the end of the line is smiling and glad they called.

You want them to feel like they are valuable to your business from the very first interaction. If you are successful in doing this over the phone, most likely, when they come into your business, they're going to come in a better state of mind and in a better mood, anticipating more of what they experienced on the phone.

Of course, a key element is to follow-up this phone interaction with a successful face-to-face interaction. When they do walk into the business, your business should be managed in such a way so they experience more of the same positivity they received on the phone.

If they had a great experience on the phone and then they walk into the door and the employee greeting them isn't smiling or enthusiastic, there's going to be a disconnect. The customer will think: What is this business really like? Are they really upbeat and positive? Do they really care about me or is this just another typical business? There will be red flags going up for the customer if there are major inconsistencies between the phone and in-person customer service.

Keeping things positive and up-beat from the phone call to the in-person greeting to any follow-up calls is a way to ensure you are promoting the best customer service possible within your business.

Benefits of a Smile in Public Speaking

In his article, "Smile, Really Smile, It's Good for Health; It's Good for Wealth[20]," Jonathan Steele, R.N., explains that a smile is one of the most effective means to capture the trust, attention and build rapport with an audience. Smiling also benefits the speaker, because it serves a natural stress-reducer and muscle-relaxer.

A smile is one of the most effective means to capture the trust, attention and build rapport with an audience.

Public speakers often arm themselves with numerous techniques and tricks for nailing a presentation, but a simple smile is an often overlooked tool that helps the speaker to put the audience at ease, leading them to be more receptive to the message. And this is true whether the audience is one or one-thousand.

Did You Know?[21]

- **Bosses are 12% more likely to promote people who smile a lot.**
- Bosses who smile at their employees are more likely to have employees who go above and beyond in their jobs.
- Smiling can create a positive work environment.

Using a Smile in Leadership

People tend to have an idea that someone in leadership should be serious, firm, in control at all times, but the truth is a good leader may be all of these things, but he or she also knows how to use a smile.

Good leaders understand the importance of creating a positive work environment, and, honestly, it's difficult to create that kind of positivity with a stern, smile-less appearance.

A smile shows employees that you support what they are doing. It creates a warmer work environment, which paves the way for improved teamwork and overall staff morale.

And we've already covered the fact that a smile is contagious. So a smile from the top dog in the company is likely to set the tone for the office, and other managers and employees will follow his or her lead.

Leadership Tip: Smile, But Don't Fake It

The attitude behind a leader's smile is most important; it isn't worth the energy to use a fake or phony smile as you try to motivate or influence your employees.

Whether you are a CEO, manager, or co-worker, a forced smile used continually may take an emotional toll over time. Business researchers label a fake smile used for business as "emotional labor."

Emotional labor can be truly exhausting not to mention ineffective when the appearance doesn't match-up with the person's true feelings or experience. It feels inauthentic to the person faking it, and the person receiving the smile picks up on the lack of authenticity as well.

Smile Through the Tears – Fake smiles vs. Real Smiles[22] addresses the seriousness of the issue:

> "*[…] faking emotions can lead to job stress, dissatisfaction and burnout. Research shows that inhibition of emotion or bottling up overworks the cardiovascular and nervous systems, and weakens the immune system. In fact, the inability to express negative emotion is one of the strongest predictors of cancer.*"

In light of this information on the importance of authentic smiles in the workplace, it makes sense for business owners and employers to seek out those candidates for jobs who have a natural tendency to be friendly and to smile.

It's difficult to take someone who doesn't have that tendency and force them to do something that is unnatural to them. This fakeness comes across to the customer loud and clear, and makes the work environment miserable for the employee.

Rather than faking a smile for the sake of positive leadership or encouraging employees to smile no matter what, the author suggests the following tips for creating a positive, healthy work environment where people actually feel like smiling:

- Create support by creating an environment were true smiles are easy.

- Create a workplace were workers can be true friends and customers come back year after year.

- Support and understand employees' pain. Don't brush over it with platitudes. Talk to them, guide them to reframe bad interactions by saying the customer was having a bad day.

- Give the employees stress-relieving options. Let them take a walk outside. Sit somewhere and do deep breathing. Create a distress room with calming colors, music and toys. Hold yoga or Tai Chi classes on site. Bring in a chair massage worker in on a regular basis.

Know the gender differences. Women smile more than men in an informal setting by an overwhelming 77% to 35% margin. Emotional labor research says women have to work even harder because as a gender we are expected to be even nicer. Women respond to stress differently. All that flight fight response research you've heard was done on men. New research shows that women like to chat and bond with other women under stress so allow them stress visiting time.

Smiling at Work

While it is clear that faking a smile or dismissing serious issues or concerns among employees are undesirable in the workplace, using genuine warmth and smiles can help to alleviate workplace stress and make the office a more pleasant place to work for everyone on staff.

A good leader knows how to spot appropriate opportunities to interject some light, tasteful humor. Let's leave the crass jokes to Steve Carell's character on The Office, but there's nothing wrong with letting some charm and a good sense of humor shine through if it is naturally part of your personality.

Sharing a laugh about a funny customer incident or chatting together about humorous family stories can lighten the mood in the office and help a leader to build rapport with employees while boosting the overall morale of the office.

And, of course, a positive mood is great for productivity, as it results in increased creativity, higher job satisfaction, and employee retention.

A Mini-Seminar: The Power of Smiling on the Job and Beyond

In our research we've come across some really excellent videos that are relevant to our topic of smiling as it pertains to the work environment and all other areas of our lives. When you have some time for a mini-seminar from the comfort of your own desk, take a look at these suggested links:

- Smile to Improve Mood on the Job: http://www.youtube.com/watch?v=OL4vIFJsIEU[23]

- Smile to Improve Your Life: http://joyousexpansion.com/blog/2011/about-spiritual-coach/spiritual-life-coach-tip-smile[24]

- The Hidden Power of Smiling: http://www.youtube.com/watch?v=U9cGdRNMdQQ

- Science of Happiness—Power of Smiling: http://www.youtube.com/watch?v=6SjOGO1tRXU[25]

Smile Stories...Lady with a Beautiful Smile

The business world is difficult with so many people applying to one position these days. I am a male corporate business owner that is an extrovert and I am also married. I look for an employee that offers a great smile along with genuine conversation. I had this one lady to come in and she didn't have a lot of experience, but she had a warm smile that could illuminate the room. I noticed that once I hired her she always kept that lovely smile on her face to greet the customers and other business associates. I was glad that I hired her because she has been with this company for many years now. That lady with the beautiful smile was my lovely mother.

Smile Stories... A Smile at the Carwash

I was at the car wash yesterday and as I watched the cars going through the system I couldn't help but notice the lethargic non-enthused, unhappy approach that each attendant adopted to undertaking their task in the production line. These people were in full view of the customers sitting watching their pride and joy being washed while trying to enjoy a coffee.

As a paying customer, should I be made to feel that I am inconveniencing the staff? Couldn't my experience have been a lot nicer with a simple smile on the faces of the attendants?

It costs nothing and is only a matter of management instilling and explaining the importance as a part of the company culture. If your staff doesn't enjoy what they're doing and can't smile, tell them to go and do something else that does make them smile, then hire someone who not only has a better attitude, but is going to contribute to the overall success of your business.

I am a firm believer that simple, FREE things like this can make a profound difference to your business and most importantly your customers experience in your business. At a time when customers have unlimited choice available on the Internet and when every dollar they spend counts, you have the power to make sure your customers and clients want to use only you...because you make them feel like they belong to you and nowhere else.

I have witnessed companies spending thousands of dollars to attract new business, only to have a non-smiling, inconvenienced attendant go up apathetically try and 'help' them, when a happy, smiling, energetic, caring attendant could have not only satisfied the customer but welded them to your business, and even better, referring new business, because you show you care.

Try it... smile tomorrow. It may even change the way you approach **your own day.**

Smile Stories… Smiling in the Face of Tragedy

I have many friends and the closest of them is a businessman. He owns a business that deals with cotton production. There are about ten branches that produce cotton and also cotton textiles. Because of the size of his business, he is one of the most significant businessmen in textile industry.

Once he faced a heartbreaking incident in the main campus of his head office. Due to an electrical problem, an accidental fire resulted. Almost the entire cotton production unit was destroyed by the unquenchable fire. The textiles that were about to be exported the next day were also completely destroyed. When he informed us, I immediately rushed to the office and helped him with the situation. We called to the fire department and somehow managed the bad situation. Even after several days, my friend was in despair thinking about the incident. Despite being consoled by his family, friends and relatives, he could not return to his normal run. After a few days, I designed a greeting card and gave it to him. The card has a saying in it.

"EVERYTHING BURNT EXCEPT FAITH & CONFIDENCE –
BUSINESS STARTS TOMORROW".

When I gave the card, he looked into my eyes after reading the saying in it. I smiled at him with an encouraging look. The moment he identified the encouraging look, he too smiled at me. Things changed from then onwards. Now he has returned back to his normal self, working towards his higher goals. The smile created a vast difference in his business.

Next

Now that we've covered the business value of smiling, let's explore how valuable smiling can be in your social life.

Chapter 3:

How Smiling Improves Your Social Life

Let us always meet each other with smile,
for the smile is the beginning of love.
Mother Teresa

In social situations of all kinds, one of the most important rules of society is to be a likeable person—someone who people enjoy; others want to be around this person. A simple smile is the most effective way to become that attractive person and to make a "likeable" first impression.

You may have a wonderful personality, but when you walk into a room without a smile, no one gets that impression. In fact, you are giving the opposite impression about yourself, which is a big mistake if you are interested in making friends, earning respect and influencing others.

A first impression is created within just a few, brief seconds.

Counter to popular opinion, what people notice most about you is not your hairstyle or your clothing…it's your smile or lack of smile that garners attention. When you walk into a room, people zoom in on your facial expression. In a few moments, they have the following internal and subconscious dialogue:

- Is he smiling?
- If not, what's wrong with him?
- Is it genuine?
- What do his teeth look like?
- What do his lips look like?

This happens on a subconscious level, so while the person may not be literally thinking these words, that's the assessment he is making.

It's a popular saying that holds so much truth

"You only get one shot at making a good first impression."

We hear it all of the time, but often dismiss it and don't really consider the gravity of it.

For this reason, a smile is one of the most powerful tools you have in your arsenal when in a situation of meeting new people in a variety of social scenarios. Your smile is paving the way for a warm, open, friendly and confident impression on others, and it is critical in the first few moments you meet others for the first time.

There's truly only one shot. Just one chance.

And then it's gone, and you are left to deal with the impact your first impression made—good or bad. We often neglect to manage those moments as we should and to maximize the opportunity to make the best first impression we can make. It is important to be continually cognizant of this social reality as we go through our day-to-day lives.

According to Maui resident and lecturer Sam Horn in her book *Concrete Confidence*[26], smiling is essential in creating a solid first impression, and in putting yourself and others at ease in that first five minutes of an interaction.

Horn writes, "The very first step to establishing a positive response in another person is to flash them a genuine, heartfelt smile… Simply said, it's hard to dislike someone who smiles at you. A smile sets up a reciprocal reaction. Recipients almost involuntarily smile back."

I personally can recall one time in which I was going about my day, not considering the impact of a first impression. I was walking into the auditorium at my church for a special after-hours program. There were individual greeters at the entrance and one of them approached me in a very friendly manner, asking if I needed directions to the auditorium. My response in that moment, my one and only first impression, was not ideal.

I must have been thinking about other things or just in an unpleasant mood, and I retorted tersely, "I know what I'm doing. I go to church here."

Immediately, the greeter's face dropped and his friendly, outgoing countenance changed. I suddenly was aware that I had made a very poor first impression. I did not smile. I was terse in my response—the first words he had ever heard leave my mouth.

Yeah, he probably thought I was a jerk!

It was a lousy first impression—not because I'm a bad guy—just because I was in a bad mood and wasn't thinking about the kind of impression I might make on people who approached me. It wasn't in the forefront of my mind, and because of that this greeter likely developed the impression that I was an unfriendly person, which really isn't true.

Looking back, the whole incident could have been turned around if I'd just smiled and said, "Thank you…I appreciate your help; I'm sorry I responded that way!"

I didn't, so it's possible to this day that the greeter sees me from time to time and recalls his negative perception of me.

What we need to understand is that we are making many first impressions throughout the day. It doesn't have to be a big event or business meeting. Entering any facility, store, school, church, etc., provides an opportunity for us to create a positive first impression by smiling.

The great thing is that a smile creates a reciprocal reaction: others smile back at you. This reaction creates more positivity in your day, so in addition to giving others an ideal impression of yourself, you are bringing more enjoyment and light to your day.

Smile Stories… My Social Life Changed

I am a single female and I work from home because I am the introvert type.

It is funny that I don't trust a lot of guys, but I did manage to make a good friend and find wonderful places to hang out at just because of a smile that I received from him at the supermarket.

He smiled at me over a joke that I had made about the fruit and I knew from then on that we were going to be friends. We go to clubs together and have drinks.

The best part is he still smiles at me every now and then to signify that he is glad that we met.

How to Be More Approachable with a Smile

Smiling is a great first step, but there are other actions to go along with your smile to create the best first impression possible. In her article, "From Wallflower to Social Butterfly,"[27] author and body language expert Patti Wood provides the following tip for appearing more approachable:

"When you enter a room, it is important to stand-up straight, smile and look around, because it gives the impression that you care about where you are, which will lead people to be more likely to approach you."

Eye contact is another component that is critical when delivering your smile. Later in the book, as we cover the different types of smiles, we will discuss the types of eye contact we recommend in each smile.

A smile is the most positive signal you can give. It reaffirms your enthusiasm and good nature, but be careful of over-grinning. Your smile is one of the strongest tools you have in meeting new people. It will help you to appear warm, open, friendly and confident, even if you are feeling on edge.[28]

-Kommersant

http://kommersant.com/p-9760/sharapova_smile_best

You will begin to see how eye contact with a smile tends to increase the sexual tension, particularly if it's lingering eye contact. Brief eye contact is going to be appropriate in most scenarios. But in situations where you want to release or dismiss any kind of potential sexual tension, then you will want the eye contact to be brief and short, if any at all.

In "The Power of Eye Contact: Your Secret for Success in Business, Love, and Life"[29] by Michael Ellsberg, we read:

If you're making eye contact with a woman, and then you smile, you'll notice an immediate release of tension. It's similar to laughter. If there's something tense going on---it can be a good tension or a bad tension, a sexual tension or a nonsexual tension--if there's laughter, that tension is going to escape. And if there's a smile, that tension is going to escape. The first person who smiles, then, is choosing to release the tension. Eye contact is something that's going to increase sexual tension, and a smile will decrease it.

p.88

We encounter social situations every day and respond to them without thinking about our smiling or lack of smiling, or eye contact and lack of eye contact. Yet, when we begin to realize the impact these behaviors make, we can gain control over our body language and begin to use it in a way to create the kinds of interactions that benefit us most, or meet our relationship objectives.

As you make an effort to appear more approachable to others, you can actually train your smile to give your face the right expression. In Chapter 10, we are going to cover methods you can utilize to work out your smile muscles and practice the types of smiles you want to use to make the most of each social situation you encounter.

Dating and Your Smile

- 86% of people say that they are more likely to strike up conversations with strangers if they are smiling.

- Virtually all Americans (99.7%) believe a smile is an important social asset.

- 96% of adults believe an attractive smile makes a person more appealing to members of the opposite sex.

It may seem obvious that a smile will make you more attractive in the dating world, but here are the statistics to back it up:

The popular website eharmony.com reveals an interesting statistic that 90% of men will not approach a woman unless he senses an inviting smile. An inviting smile often gives them the courage that they will not have to face rejection—which is a common fear for many men.

A welcoming smile from a woman gives the man a green light to approach her, so he can put aside the overwhelming fear of rejection.

This is helpful insight for women who are trying to succeed in the dating world or find that special someone. It's even helpful information for a woman who does not want to attract interest or be approached by men. The type of smile you give will send a certain message to the opposite sex.

If you want to be approached, by all means show an inviting smile. If this is not your desire, keep those kinds of smiles to yourself.

Because we know a smile makes a face more attractive to others, it makes sense that it influences whether or not someone is interested in you for a romantic relationship.

> It has reinforced one of my guiding principles that we really are in charge of our destinies. We do have influence over the things that happen to us by virtue of our actions. **Smiling is a case in which a simple act can have profound effects on the kinds of experiences we have with other people and how they treat us.**[30]
>
> –Richard Manly, Go Ahead and Smile

We saw this chart below in chapter two but I think it is very import to ask ourselves these questions again in relationship to our social life.

The Sexy Smile Survey: What does it mean to you?

Dale Jorgenson

When asked, *"What is the first thing you notice in a person's smile?"* The most common responses were:

- Straightness
- Whiteness & Color of Teeth
- Cleanliness of Teeth
- Sincerity of Smile
- Any Missing Teeth?
- Sparkle of Smile

And when asked, *"What types of things do you consider make a smile unattractive?"* the most common responses were:

- Discolored, Yellow, or Stained Teeth
- Missing Teeth
- Crooked Teeth
- Decaying Teeth & Cavities
- Gaps & Spaces in Teeth
- Dirty Teeth

It's easy to see from this survey from Kommersant that getting teeth in good condition is essential to creating a beautiful smile that can be a true asset in social situations.

ScienceDaily.com explained in its article "Men Look for Good Bodies in Short-Term Mates, Pretty Faces in Long-Term Mates"[31] that facial beauty is a key factor men in particular consider for long-term relationships: "Men's priorities shift depending on what they want in a mate, with facial features taking on more importance when a long-term relationship is the goal."

So a smile in itself—particularly an inviting smile—will help you to create "long-term relationship" potential in the eyes of men. If you are searching for a mate for the long-haul, making an effort to smile as much as possible will work to your benefit.

Oral Hygiene and the Impact on Your Smile

Imagine walking into a room with straight, strong posture, smiling as you look around the room. Now imagine doing this while having really bad breath or bad teeth. It's easy to see how these oral hygiene issues can decrease the effectiveness of using your smile to influence others, particularly when it comes to dating.

It is important to do the best with what you have, but there are certain situations that require a bit more attention, so you can make the most of your first impressions. If your oral hygiene is bad, then no matter what you do—dimming the lights, turning candles on, wearing perfume, playing romantic music in the background—it will be difficult for you to overcome the problem that comes with poor oral hygiene, including unattractive teeth and bad breath.

The Sexy Smile Survey (*Kommersant*) revealed that people believe a clean mouth is most important to maintaining a healthy relationship. A good healthy smile with nice, bright teeth not only feels good and enables the person to display more confidence, but it is more attractive to people, particularly significant others.

While you may have not previously considered how important good oral hygiene is to your relationships and potential relationships, it may be a game-changer for you to understand that it may be the single most important factor in these relationships.

This survey showed that nearly 59% of the people said they would be most disturbed if their significant other was not brushing or flossing his or her teeth on a regular basis. In fact, they said oral hygiene was more important than that the person wearing deodorant.

Who would have thought B.O. was more tolerable than stinky breath?

By giving your oral hygiene the attention it needs, you can go a long way toward improving your relationships with others and even attracting the attention of a love interest.

While good dental care can help to enhance your smile, one common cosmetic procedure may take away from your smile's effectiveness in social situations.

Smile Video Resources

We recommend the following videos about smiling to further your understanding about what happens when you smile and how you can use this essential facial expression to put your best face forward in all social situations.

Understanding Characteristics of Different Facial Expressions:
http://www.youtube.com/watch?v=LHraznv4pHQ&feature=related[32]

What a Smile Says about Who You Are:
   http://www.youtube.com/watch?v=yNusttI9MyU[33]

The Duchenne Smile:
   http://www.youtube.com/watch?v=y3_bk9jHXrI[34]

Many people, particularly women, are beginning to use Botox to create a youthful appearance, but some evidence is emerging that this procedure can negatively impact one's smile. Botox has the potential to prevent the elevator muscles from elevating the corners of the eye as they should during a genuine smile.

In other words, Botox can potentially mute a smile so that it isn't as impactful as it could be without the cosmetic procedure. While crow's feet around the eyes may be diminished, the impact of the smile can be diminished as well, so it is important to consider this result when thinking about using Botox.

Because a smile brings with it so much power for influencing and attracting others, it is likely even more important than maintaining a perfectly youthful look. In a society obsessed by youthfulness, this issue can be unfortunately overlooked.

Society's opinion on cosmetic procedures may change over time, yet the power of the smile is universal and timeless.

Outside of dating and attracting romantic relationships, a smile provides the opportunity to shine in any social situation or environment.

When two people in conversation with one another use the same kind of body movements and gestures, including a smile, they will naturally experience greater empathy for each other on a subconscious level.

According to an article entitled simply "Smile" 65% of communication is non-verbal, and the smile remains as the strongest communication tool. It can be used for the most good possible, when the person knows how to use the smile correctly to achieve the optimal social results.

Think for a moment how you feel when someone smiles at you. Whether it is at the grocery store or at your place of work, smiling puts people at ease. When someone smiles at you, it is nearly impossible not to return the smile. It is a natural reaction to smile when you receive a smile.

The primary reason a smile is so effective is because smiling enables you to reflect good to another person. A smile makes you feel better about yourself and makes you more attractive, and someone returning the smile to you has the same effect. Once you begin this smile chain-reaction, you receive a big emotional boost—whether you think about it or not.

In his article "Share Yourself and Your Wisdom with the World: Smile,"[35] Rabbi Boruch Leff explains the great power that comes with a teeth-bearing smile:

No matter what the circumstance, even during times of stress and hardship, it is possible to look inside ourselves to find a reason to smile.

When we open our mouths and smile at someone we are communicating the following message: "I want to show you what is inside of me." When we smile and display our teeth, we are showing others that there's a lot inside that we want to share.... Whether we realize it or not, when we smile we are showing a glimpse of our wisdom. God created us so that when we are happy we smile, we laugh, we show our teeth. This is as if to say, "I am in a wonderful mood. I feel the grandeur of life. I am happy to be alive in this world. Thus, I am showing my teeth to the world – and through my teeth, I am displaying my wisdom. I have a precious role to play in this world by tapping into and utilizing my wisdom and sharing it with others. This is why I'm smiling; this is the reason I am showing you my teeth.

Smile Stories... A Better Romantic Life

About 6 years ago I was working on a cruise ship as an entertainer. About half way through my act a lady in the crowd caught my eye. I smiled at her, and gave a sly wink, before continuing with the show.

Afterwards, while having a beer at the bar with the rest of my band the lady came over to speak to me. She had seen me performing many years earlier, a budding guitarist, and she told me she'd recognized me purely based on my smile.

Today, we are happily married with two beautiful children, a boy and a girl, and to this day I am glad that she caught my eye that day on the ship.

Whether you are a pro at smiling or struggle to smile throughout your day, this passage proves how a simple smile can open up opportunities to sharing and connecting with others. As we consider ways to better relate to others, it is impossible to achieve the relational success we desire in all areas of our lives without making an effort to let our smiles shine.

A smile can make others feel that we appreciate and like them and also disarms tension in times of conflict. How can someone be angry at you, when you are genuinely smiling? It makes it much more difficult for negative emotions to remain when a smile is brought into the situation.

Still, we must emphasize that a true genuine smile is the one that will achieve the most benefit and desired social results. We've all known someone with a fake smile. Obviously, in most situations, a fake smile is a big turn-off, so it is important to allow our smile to come from a true place of joy and happiness in our lives.

No matter what the circumstance, even during times of stress and hardship, it is possible to look inside ourselves to find a reason to smile.

In his book *About Face*,[36] Dan Hill explains the importance of avoiding a fake smile that feigns happiness. He discusses how facial coders have actually identified a fake "social smile," which is characterized as an expression that gives itself away by using fewer facial muscles to form.

While the people around you may not be expert "facial coders," they likely have enough social awareness to detect a fake smile when they see one. Avoid this problem all together by sharing your smile from a place of true happiness. In any situation, we must identify what gives us joy in life and create facial expressions that come from that place.

Using Your Duchenne Smile for Maximum Impact

"What is a Duchenne smile?" Here's your answer:

"A Duchenne smile contracts the zygomatic muscle [the muscle that runs from the corner of your mouth to the top of your jaw] of the cheek and eye, forming crow's feet. The crow's feet indicate that the smile is genuine and that the smiler is truly happy. It was discovered by and is named after Guillaume Duchenne—a French neurologist."[37]

Pshychologist Paul Ekman, who studied facial structure and smiling, found that producing the Duchenne smile can actually bring about a sense of "euphoria, happiness, joy and genuine well-being".[38]

This natural, genuine smile is accompanied by increased brain activity in the part of the brain responsible for positive emotions. This is great news for people who struggle to smile or have a tendency to use a fake smile. Ekman found you can activate this pleasure center in your brain by putting a Duchenne smile on your face.

This is a good example of the popular phrase "faking it 'til you make it!" While you may not feel like smiling, you can create happiness in your brain by using this type of smile.

See the third video in the Smile Video Resources to see a presentation regarding the Duchenne smile.

Is there Such Thing as a Lying Smile?

A fake smile, also identified as a lying smile, can create negative emotions and lead to problematic social behavior. Ekman, along with authors Friesen and O'Sullivan explained the issue of a lying smile and how it impacts the impressions we create when we use it.

The authors analyzed the subtle differences found in people who were truthful and those who were lying about experiencing pleasant feelings; in other words, they had a fake or lying smile. They identified lying smiles as those that featured traces of muscular actions associated with disgust, fear, contempt, or sadness.

These subjects may have had a "happy mask," but their facial expressions were revealing a different message regarding what was really going on with their emotions.

Other characteristics of people using lying smiles include:

- Excessively touching their faces.

- Engaging in nervous ticks, such as scratching their noses when speaking.

- Giving a half-hearted smile with just their mouths, while their eyes gave a negative message.

Being aware of the negative impacts of a fake or lying smile is important to consider as you strive to utilize a smile to your benefit in social situations. If this is a struggle for you, you can practice on getting in touch with the positive things happening in your life, so you can achieve a Duchenne smile that creates happiness in your life and speaks happiness to others.

Once you do this, your tendency to give a fake smile will diminish, and thus you will begin the positive chain-reaction of smiling, which is the ultimate goal of this journey.

In light of this, it is safe to say that walking around in our day-to-day lives without a smile is not the kind of life God wants or expects from us. If this is a struggle for you, identify the places and the people in your life who bring a smile to your face and make you laugh. Go to those places of laughter and avoid the people and places that work to steal your joy.

People want to be around others who have a deep happiness and joy, and this is the kind of joy that relationship with God brings to our lives. It creates an attractiveness that no cosmetic surgery or even great dental work can provide.

A true, genuine smile must come from deep within. We've discussed in this chapter how a shallow, fake smile can bring about negative emotions—and this is not going to serve us well in social situations.

There is indeed great power in the smile, and when we can begin to get in touch with joy and happiness in our lives, we can let that joy shine through to the world through our smiles.

Whether you seek a romantic relationship or just want to have a more active and enjoyable social life, you are in control of the situation when you can grasp the impact your smile can make in your life.

What Your Smile Says About You[39]

From *Smile! The secret science of smiling,* the author shares five things your smile tells others about you:

1. **Sensitivity** – a smile lets the person you are conversing with know that you are sensitive and in tune with what they are saying.

2. **Maturity** – smiling conveys a sense of maturity because if you can smile at times when you least feel the desire to smile, you show maturity and growth as a person. You are letting people know that even in the hard times, you value a positive attitude above the irrational

3. **Assurance** – a warm smile tells people that you value them and that you are in fact listening to what they have to say. So, smile and be genuinely interested in the people around you.

4. **Leverage** – leverage sounds a bit manipulative, but I don't mean it in that sense. A smile makes you much more approachable and therefore you are more likable. If closer relationships with your family or the people you work with are what you desire, try smiling more openly.

Smile Stories… Beating Bullying

I was bullied in school. It started when I was only six or seven years old. My parents always told me to shake it off and keep smiling so that's what I did. Sometimes the bullying got the worst of me and I fought back but mostly I tried to remember what my parents had said. Almost everyone in my class bullied me, except a few, and those few were bullied themselves.

Many years later, when I was 20, I was at a party in a town a couple of hours from where I lived and I was on a balcony having a cigarette. There was another person there, a boy, who I recognized but couldn't place. After a while he looked at me and just smiled, he didn't say anything. I asked him what he was smiling about and he asked me if I remembered him. He was one of the boys in my class who was bullied as well and he told me that he was inspired by my smile in school, that he was able to keep his faith up that things would get better, because of my smile.

We talked through the night and after that party we fell in love and became boyfriend and girlfriend. A smile can do so much.

Smile Stories… A Buffet of Smiles

About three years ago I was on vacation at a resort with my friends. We were having dinner at a buffet restaurant. I got up several times to fill my plate with the wonderful dishes they were serving. On one of such trips I came across a man I had never seen before. I was happy and relaxed and I smiled at him and he gave me a warm smile back.

Later that night, I was waiting for the valet to bring our car around and this man came up to me and said, "Thank you for smiling at me, you made my heart smile." I thought, "Wow, a smile is really powerful."

Smile Stories… Six Words That Changed a Life

Six words, "Smile…it can't be that bad" changed Judy's life. Judy is a young woman I worked with some years ago. She was in her late twenties, maybe early thirties, more than a little overweight, and not the most stylish dresser. What was most striking about her appearance was her smile; it was always there. Anyone passing Judy in the hallway was greeted with that smile and a soft, "Hello," or, "Good Morning," in her gentle, Minnesota accent.

I happened to be with Judy one day when she had her driver's license out of her purse. The photograph on her license showed a face that looked like it had never smiled! The corners of her mouth were turned down, her face looked slack, and the eyes were dark and troubled. The overall impression was anger and deep grief.

"Whoa! Judy…is that really you? What in the world was going on? You look like you're mad at the world!" Judy giggled. "Yes, it's me. I used to look like that all the time."

She then shared with me her story and the six words that changed her life. Judy had moved to Tennessee to care for an invalid uncle. Her life revolved around caring for this much older and very ill man who, though grateful, offered little in the way of good company for a shy young woman. When he died, Judy realized for the first time that she had nothing - no job skills, no education, no experience with which to support herself, and no friends.

Lonely, grieving, and terrified, she took a big step and enrolled in a community college CAD/CAM program. The Judy that walked the halls between classes was the Judy captured in her driver's license photo. She didn't talk, didn't smile, didn't make eye contact.

One day, however, she met an instructor in the hallway who, in passing, said, "Smile...it can't be that bad." As Judy told me the story, she giggled again. "I was so embarrassed! And I didn't say anything at all. I couldn't. But I started thinking... maybe he was right."

Nothing in Judy's life had changed, but she made a decision to smile anyway, to put a smile on her face without waiting for it to spontaneously show up. And so she did. She would arrive at school and, very self-consciously at first, put a smile on her face as she walked across the parking lot. She forced herself to look up at the people she met, even if only for an instant. Over and over she repeated to herself the six words that started her down the path: "Smile...it can't be that bad."

Without realizing it, she said, she had begun to practice "fake it 'till you make it," acting happy even when she wasn't. "And when I did," she said, "things changed. People stopped avoiding me. Before, people sometimes crossed the halls to walk on the other side, and if they didn't, I did. When I started smiling, even though I didn't really feel it, people reacted differently. It took a little while, but one morning, someone actually said hello to me. And I smiled for real!"

Judy later went to the instructor who had made the comment and thanked him. As you might expect, he was surprised that his almost throwaway comment had that kind of impact. Judy met his family, visited his church, and slowly developed a social network. After living in Tennessee for more than ten years, she made her first friends.

When she told me the story, she finished with, "See? You never know how you might influence someone with what you say. Those six words changed my life. When I started acting happy, I became happy. I didn't even know it was happening, but it was, and I'm so glad he told me to, 'Smile...it can't be that bad.' He was right...it wasn't that bad...and it won't ever be that bad again."

Age 43, Female

Smile Stories... It's the Little Things

I was talking to a friend when he was having an argument with his girlfriend, and he was on the verge of breaking up with her. During our talk, something silly happened (I dropped someone's drink on him) and I cracked a big smile but trying not to laugh because I knew how hurt he was and now drenched in a vodka/cranberry. I let it slip by accident and smiled ear to ear and followed with a little chuckle.

He looked as though he was really angry and then smiled too. The next thing he said was, "Thank you for making me realize it is the little things she does that make me happy" and that came from a smile.

Smile Stories... Young Love Returns

When I was ten years old, I had a girlfriend. She was very cute and lovely girl. I always liked talking with her – even during class. We were in school together for three years. Then my father got a transfer and my family moved about an hour from our home. We started our new life there. Sixteen years later, my father got transferred again – this time back home. In the meantime I had finished college. I had a good job in a good company, and started settling into my life.

One of my neighbors became ill and was admitted to a hospital. I went to visit him there. I saw a girl wearing a nurse uniform and smiling at me. I walked up to her and asked why she was smiling at me. She said, "There's nothing wrong with smiling at someone you know."

I wondered what she meant. Later I learned that she was my childhood girlfriend! We started a new relationship and became lovers, then a married couple. Today we are well settled and have a child. All this happened because of her cute smile. I now recognize the value of a smile in each and everyone's life.

If One Person Smiles[40]

There was this article in the *New Yorker* I read a long time ago and came across again recently about people who choose to end their lives plunging from the Golden Gate bridge. This happens at a rate of about once every two weeks or so, though these events rarely make the news, as law enforcement and the media have mutually agreed to play down the incidents because they don't want to encourage suicide by glorifying the act.

The article includes a story by a Dr. Jerome Motto, who recounts a particularly sobering bridge suicide occurring sometime in the 1970s.

Dr. Motto: "I went to this guy's apartment afterward with the assistant medical examiner… The guy was in his thirties, lived alone, pretty bare apartment. He'd written a note and left it on his bureau. It said, "I'm going to walk to the bridge. If one person smiles at me on the way, I will not jump."

One smile, one "hello", one door held open might not save someone's life. But it might. In a world where it seems that everyone blends with the crowd and it's incredibly easy to go unnoticed, I smile and look at everyone in the eyes that passes me by just because of that article. Sometimes people are so preoccupied in their minds that when I smile at them and nod my head hello, I get ignored. A couple times people don't smile back. But then there are the few who smile warmly and you can feel a thank you wash over their face toward you without even having to say the words.

It breaks my heart that a few suicides could have been prevented if a stranger smiled at them just for a brief second as they passed each other on a busy train. Just to feel a connection to this world. To not feel invisible. Even more so that people actually feel nobody sees them at all. But I do. I do see you, and I smile. Every awkward look back, or mean face somebody gives me that doesn't want a welcomed smile is worth coming across somebody who actually needs it. Especially when a lot of us, suicidal or not, probably needed it that day.

I will always be that one person that smiles.

Smile Stories… Smiling At Strangers

I can't help it. Maybe I want people to like me too much, but I'm also guilty. I smile at strangers! It feels like what civilization (is it?) expects of us, is to just be indifferent. If you walk on the sidewalk, you should at all times keep a straight face, mind your own business, don't look people in the eye...

A few months back I worked in the city and I had to drive to work in lots of traffic - something new, as I normally work in a small town. After a while a saw that the sidewalk rules also apply to the traffic. People are just too hasty to get to where they are going. Except for the one day, a guy drove behind me. He smiled the whole time and it was just so contagious! My day just looked a lot brighter.

I just can't help but wonder what he was smiling about for half an hour?

Maybe he's also just a Person that Smile at Strangers!

Smile Stories... No Longer Scared To Smile

For the past two weeks I've slowly begun to smile at strangers often. Whenever a stranger makes eye contact with me, most of the time, I smile at them. I used to never smile at strangers because of fear, but now I make a conscious effort to. Sometimes people don't smile back, but sometimes they do, and may even greet me. There are times when I smile at a stranger, that I can tell they really appreciate it, and are happy to have received a smile from me. It's so rewarding to be able to brighten a person's mood just with a smile. I decided to start smiling at people because I tend to be very shy, and I want to be able to come off as more friendly and open to people.

The only time I tend not to smile at people is with certain type of guys around my age. With those types of guys, I'm scared that if I smile at them, they'll take it as a sign of flirtation. And then that'll make me nervous (I'm no good with guys). So yeah, I don't smile at them for that reason. But besides that, I'll smile at pretty much everyone.

Smile Stories... The Magic of Life

The smile only comes when my heart awakens. It is when my joy paints sunshine on my face. My smile is the windows of the soul that opens to receive what life can offer the best. It is the music that my soul sings several times for life and lives and never, never tiring my day. It is what remains when the last hope tells me that something needs to be done by myself, putting shining stars in my mouth...It is the magic of life that makes me to love to smile.

Smile Stories... Lexi and Michael

LEXI, an unhappy woman of substance, sits impatiently on a bus stop bench. MICHAEL, a (great looking, well built, bald) homeless guy, sits down next to her with a big smile on his face.

LEXI: What are you smiling for?

MICHAEL: It's what I do.

LEXI: I won't ask.

MICHAEL: I sell smiles for a living.

LEXI: I'm not interested.

MICHAEL: Here, have a free one - on me. (He smiles at her.)

LEXI: No thank you.

MICHAEL: Sorry, can't take it back. You'll have to give it to someone else.

LEXI: What?

MICHAEL: The smile. You'll have to give it away if you don't want it. Or sell it if you like - apparently it hasn't been used much.

LEXI: What do you mean by that?

MICHAEL: You don't smile very often, do you?

LEXI: So what if I don't?

MICHAEL: Shouldn't waste your smile... there are plenty of people who could use one.

LEXI: Well they can have mine.

MICHAEL: Your what?

LEXI: My smile.

MICHAEL: I don't see one.

LEXI: I thought you just gave me one.

MICHAEL: I tried, but it didn't stick. I think it bounced right off.

LEXI: Fine. What's there to smile about anyway?

MICHAEL: Well--

LEXI: You don't have to answer that.

MICHAEL: There are lots of things to smile about. It's a beautiful day outside; the buses are running on time--

LEXI: I don't want to hear about it.

MICHAEL: --and look at that flower over there, now that would make anybody smile--

LEXI: Would you leave me alone! (A long moment of silence. Finally, she gives in.)

LEXI: So what's the going rate on smiles these days?

MICHAEL: Pardon me?

LEXI: Your smiles...how much are they?

MICHAEL: Oh, they're very expensive.

LEXI: So's my taste.

MICHAEL: You probably couldn't afford one.

LEXI: Try me.

MICHAEL: I'm warning...it'll cost you.

LEXI: Yes, I know, HOW MUCH?

MICHAEL: One smile.

LEXI: One smile?

MICHAEL: That's how much they cost.

LEXI: What?

MICHAEL: The price for a smile is exactly one smile. That's the going rate. (She thinks about it.)

LEXI: Alright. (smiles) I'll take one.

MICHAEL: It was a pleasure doing business with you.(he leaves)(Daisy, a streetwalker, sits down next to her.)

DAISY: What's with the smile?

LEXI: I sell smiles for a living.

This story is to remind you to always smile and be cheerful! It makes people happy! Keep on smiling!

Next

Smiling definitely improves your social life. Let's take a look at the psychology behind it.

Chapter 4:

How Smiling Helps Your Mental Health

*He smiled understandingly-much more than understandingly.
It was one of those rare smiles with a quality of eternal
reassurance in it that you may come across four or five times
in life. It faced--or seemed to face--the whole external world
for an instant, and then concentrated on you with an irresistible
prejudice in your favor. It understood you just as far as you
wanted to be understood, believed in you as you would like to
believe in yourself.*
– **F. Scott Fitzgerald**, *The Great Gatsby*

A smile can say a lot about your gender, personality and psychological make-up. It has the power to send messages to others without need for an actual word. Think of a loving mother's smile and the many words it speaks to her children and what it says about her personality. Then, there's the smile from someone who knows you so well, they know what you are thinking without you needing to speak a word.

The type of smile you have—and how your teeth are displayed in your mouth when you smile—also speak to your gender—the femininity and masculinity of your appearance. All of this plays a predominant role in the psychological aspects of your smile.

Are you surprised to learn that your teeth influence your gender perception? The shape of your teeth and the length of your teeth can cause your face to look more feminine or more masculine.

Here's the break-down on how your lateral incisors—the teeth on either side of your center teeth—have distinct characteristics, giving you a gender-specific appearance:

- Lateral incisors that are small in size make your smile appear more feminine.

- Larger lateral incisors make your face appear more masculine or feminine depending on the length, size and shape.

- Slightly-tilted lateral incisors appear more feminine.

- Straight lateral incisors appear more masculine.

- Lateral incisors with rounded edges and are shorter than the middle teeth appear feminine.

- Lateral incisors that are the same length as middle teeth appear more masculine.

- Lateral incisors that are more triangular in shape and narrower at the gum line look more feminine.

- Side teeth that are squarer in shape look more masculine.

Another set of teeth that have been identified as influencers of personality and gender include the canines. Here's what we know:

- Canine teeth—also known as fang teeth—have been representative of a carnivore since the days of the caveman.

- Prominent canine teeth that are larger and longer than other teeth point to an aggressive personality.

- Canine teeth that blend in with the other teeth—being similar size—point to a more agreeable personality.

- Canine teeth with pointed tips are associated with people who have a dominant personality.

- Canine teeth with rounded tips are associated with people who possess a passive personality.

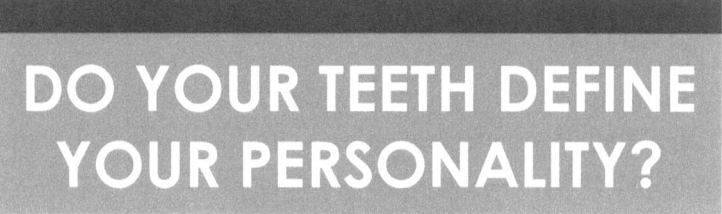

DO YOUR TEETH DEFINE YOUR PERSONALITY?

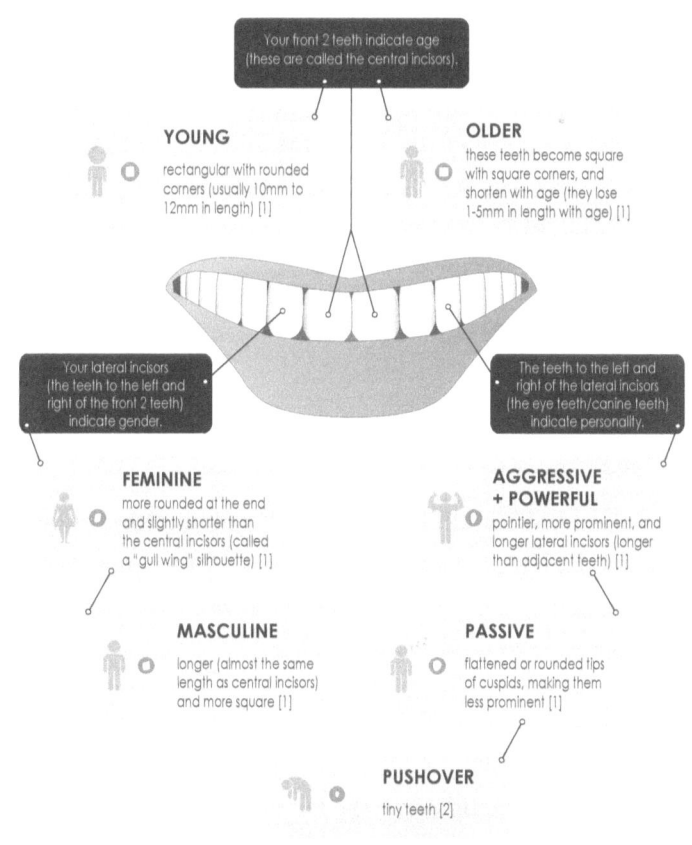

Your front 2 teeth indicate age (these are called the central incisors).

YOUNG
rectangular with rounded corners (usually 10mm to 12mm in length) [1]

OLDER
these teeth become square with square corners, and shorten with age (they lose 1-5mm in length with age) [1]

Your lateral incisors (the teeth to the left and right of the front 2 teeth) indicate gender.

The teeth to the left and right of the lateral incisors (the eye teeth/canine teeth) indicate personality.

FEMININE
more rounded at the end and slightly shorter than the central incisors (called a "gull wing" silhouette) [1]

AGGRESSIVE + POWERFUL
pointier, more prominent, and longer lateral incisors (longer than adjacent teeth) [1]

MASCULINE
longer (almost the same length as central incisors) and more square [1]

PASSIVE
flattened or rounded tips of cuspids, making them less prominent [1]

PUSHOVER
tiny teeth [2]

*Carrington College (2011). Do teeth define your personality? –
INFOGRAPHIC. Infographics Archive | Infographic Website Offering Infographics
and Data Visualization. Retrieved January 21, 2013, from http://www.
infographicsarchive.com/interesting-facts/do-teeth-define-your-personality/*

*What does all of this "teeth talk" mean to you and the psychological
implications of your smile?*

Cosmetic dental procedures now make it possible for you
to design a smile to help you express the traits you find desirable.
Sometimes, Mother Nature is a bit unfair, and we find ourselves with
smiles that give people a negative or untrue impression of who we are.

Because the first impression is so essential to one's image and
others' perceptions of us when it comes to relationships, business and
life in general, it can be worth one's time and money to go for dental
procedures to optimize your smile and ensure you are delivering the
impression you desire.

> When you're smiling…keep on smiling…The whole
> world smiles with you.
>
> **Frank Sinatra**

For example, rounding out pointed canine teeth can be helpful
for the individual who does not want to give the impression of an
aggressive personality. Or tilted lateral incisors can be straightened to
go from a feminine to more masculine smile.

Cosmetic Dentistry Help

Thanks to cosmetic dentistry it's no longer necessary to settle
for a less than desirable smile or one that takes away from the type of
image you want to project to others.

When you can take the steps to achieve the teeth that agree with your true personality type, you will begin to feel more comfortable in your skin, which can only enhance your people-skills.

However, if you are ready to consider cosmetic dental work, it is important to find a cosmetic dentist who is very informed about how teeth impact your appearance and communication.

In addition to being knowledgeable about issues related to teeth and personality, the ideal dentist will be able to help you achieve your appearance goals while ensuring you maintain optimal teeth functioning.

It would be a shame to look great, while having teeth that do not chew properly or cause jaw problems down the road.

Don't be afraid to interview cosmetic dentists and ask the necessary questions to determine if they have the knowledge and skills to help you meet your objectives.

The Psychological Impact of Smiling

While we usually think happiness is the source of a smile, at times the act of smiling itself can create happiness. In his book, *Happiness: The Science Behind Your Smile*,[41] author Daniel Nettle explains that the secret science in smiling is how you can create happiness within yourself by faking a smile.

This may seem bizarre, but the act of smiling releases hormones, neurotransmitters and endorphins that actually make you feel happy. As it ends up, the popular saying, "Fake it 'til you make it" holds some truth to it after all.

Smiling, although you may not feel like it, can elevate your mood and create a spark of happiness. It may feel unnatural or fake to begin smiling when you do not feel happy, but just forcing yourself to get out there and do it can make a big difference.

What began as a forced, shallow smile can become a genuine facial expression creating positive change in your mind.

This doesn't mean you have to walk around with a fake smile on your face day in and day out, but it may be something you can try in your car on the way home from work, or in the morning before you start your day.

No one has to see you attempting the "fake it 'til you make it" smile, but by doing it in private you can reap the mood-enhancing brain benefits the smile has to offer you. In fact, you may discover that "faking it" in private will cause you to smile more naturally without forcing it as you continue with your day.

Fake It 'Til You Make It Experiment

The next time you are feeling down in the dumps or wake up in a funk, try this simple smile experiment to see if you can give your endorphins a much-needed boost:

1. Make an effort to smile first thing in the morning.

2. Smile in the shower, or while you are brewing your coffee.

3. As you are getting ready and looking in the mirror, smile at your reflection.

4. Take note of how your mood is throughout the day. Does it seem to improve after smiling?

Do you find yourself smiling more often throughout the day without "forcing" it?

Barry Neil Kaufman explains in his book, *Happiness is a Choice*, that our lives can improve greatly when we decide to be happy no matter what the circumstances.

Many people live life in such a way that they only experience happiness when everything is going well. But when you choose happiness regardless of what is going on around you, your life is fuller, more satisfying and the positivity you possesses reaches others who are likely to respond to you in a more positive way.

Your self-confidence and self-esteem naturally increases, because others are responding to you more positively.

In his book *Stress Management*,[42] Jeff Gero, PhD, shares experiences from his Stress Management Program utilized for executives in corporations. He explains how he instructs participants to look into the mirror when things are stressful. He then instructs them to smile and allow the smile to grow into a laugh.

Gero explains that this process automatically sends a message to the brain that everything is okay again, which then produces endorphins and other positive hormones, off-setting the negative impact of daily stress.

This same application is effective when people are going through any kind of stress or life challenge. We cannot control things that come along in life, such as being in accidents, floods, or experiencing other tragic events. However, we can control how we respond.

Responding with a smile enables people to get through a variety of difficult times in a more positive place.

When you choose happiness, you regain a sense of control over your life and a sense of control regarding the way others respond to you in your life. Once you can begin to realize this, it is very enlightening and powerful.

Smiling and Endorphins: What Does This Mean for You?

We briefly touched on the fact that smiling actually releases endorphins into the blood stream, but you may be wondering exactly what this means.

Endorphins are chemicals, or a type of neurotransmitter, produced in the brain in response to a variety of stimuli. Scientists discovered endorphins in 1975 and found that they function within the transmissions of signals as part of the nervous system.

The two most common factors that cause the release of endorphins are stress and pain, but smiling is also known to be a big influencer on endorphin release. Here's how the feel-good endorphins function within your brain:

- Endorphins interact with the brain's opiate receptors to reduce our pain perception, working in a similar way as morphine works in the body.

- With endorphins, the activation of the opiate receptors is a natural process that does not lead to addiction.

- Research has shown that a true smile can produce a pain tolerance analgesic in our body that lasts for 20 to 30 minutes.

- Smiling releases endorphins into the blood stream, leading to enhanced mood.

- Endorphins help to reduce stress hormones, such as cortisol.

- These endorphins are released by the act of smiling, whether you truly feel like smiling or not!

Give Me a Reason to Smile!

Perhaps you are not a naturally "smiley" person and need more evidence to be convinced that smiling is really worth your time and effort. Check this out:

- Smiling brightens your own mood and the mood of those around you.

- It is much more difficult to be angry at someone who is smiling.

- Smiling can be a stress reducer in difficult situations.

- Smiling leads to more favorable impressions of the people around us; people are funnier, more enjoyable, more entertaining when we ourselves have a smile on our face.

- When we are smiling and laughing, new, healthy cell production increases.

- A smile elevates antibody levels in the blood and saliva, which increases immunity and improves health.

…Smiling is not only a step towards health and happiness
but a step towards world peace.

When you consider all of these benefits, it becomes easier to see how powerful your smile can be. It's no wonder why studies have shown that negative people are more likely to get sick often or have health-related problems.

Reading Emotions and Deceit through Facial Expressions[43]

In this video, Cliff Lansley, Director of Emotional Intelligence Academy, shares how we can learn a lot about others through micro and subtle facial expressions.

The video provides some helpful insight regarding the power of our facial expressions and smiles as well as how we can understand others:

http://www.youtube.com/watch?v=RnwdndsspTI&feature=related

Furthermore, it's not a stretch to say that smiling is not only a step towards health and happiness but a step towards world peace.

People who are healthier and happier and who view those around them in a more positive light, can't help but be a more peaceful people.

The fact that a smile is universal makes it a form of communication anyone from any part of the world can understand. If you were dropped right in the middle of a foreign country, your smile could enable you to communicate with others, while boosting your own mood and self-confidence.

You may want to think twice about purchasing the latest supplement or miracle drug; smiling is free and effective! It positively impacts both your psychological and physical well-being as well as your social interactions.

In *Smile! The Secret Science of Smiling*[44], Author Elan Sun Star describes what she learned from "Dr. F" who conducted research on the social benefits of smiling. She shared:

> *I asked Dr. F if there was one element that really stood out in her research to show the beneficial social effects of smiling. She said, "I think the most important thing is to have a better, healthier sense of social awareness. In other words, when people are smiling and have that type of positive emotion, they generally think in terms of 'we.' thus they can negotiate around differences of opinion, but instead of thinking 'me and you' or 'me against you,' they're thinking, 'we,' and I think that is a very important thing to remember.*
>
> *It sort of implies what we have in common and not our differences, and that helps to unite us, rather than divide us— and I think smiling does this really well. (p.124)*

The Benefits of Smiling During Hard Times

When difficult, sad or even tragic times come, smiling may be the last thing you feel like doing. However, research tells us that smiling—even when you may not feel like it—can actually help you to get through the hard times.

In *Smile Through the Tears – Fake Smiles Vs. Real Smiles*[45], Author Patti Wood explains the fact that there is a two way street between pleasure centers in the brain and facial muscles. This means that just putting our face into a smile, even when we aren't *feeling* happy, sends signals to the brain, releasing the feel-good endorphins into the blood stream.

Wood goes onto describe how the brain circuitry is set-up to respond positively to a smile, so when you make the effort to smile, you are improving your own mood as well as making others around you smile.

Below are some difficult life situations in which smiling can be a benefit:

Coping with Chronic Illness

A smile and laughter have been shown to boost the immune system, which is obviously a big help to people who are suffering from chronic illness. Whether you are facing an illness or you are trying to be there for a friend or family member who is ill, don't be afraid to tell jokes or act silly.

People facing illnesses and disease need to smile and laugh. It can be a restorative and healing time for them to get their minds off the illness and enjoy the simplicity of some smiles and laughter.

Often people who are sick, specifically those facing terminal illnesses feel like people are walking on egg shells around them, afraid to seem too happy or to appear like they are inconsiderate to their situation. The truth is that even people who are facing death need to have moments of "lightness" and happiness.

As we discussed earlier, a smile can provide relaxation, stress-relief, a boost to one's mood—all things that someone who is sick needs in their life.

The book entitled *Choosing to Smile*[46] was written by three friends, Julie Houlker, Michelle Rickaby and Glenda Standeven—each of them battling cancer. As they shared the stories of their lives through the book, they also shared with the readers how important it was for them to remain optimistic and continue to create happiness in their lives, even during the difficult health situations they faced.

Whether it is watching a comedy, sharing funny stories or just sharing a smile, you can bring joy into your life and the lives of others who may be facing chronic illnesses.

Facing Depression

A Psychology Today article, *Happily Ever Laughter*[47] addresses how laughter can benefit depressed people. The author explains that years of research have provided information, revealing how significant the impact is that laughter can have for people facing depression:

- In a study of depressed and suicidal senior citizens, patients who were able to recover were the ones who showed a sense of humor.

- People with high stress levels who also had a sense of humor were less-depressed than those with high stress levels with little sense of humor.

- Students who utilized humor as a coping tool were more likely to have a positive mood.

While not all depression is curable with laughter and smiling, there is plenty of reason to believe that a smile can boost one's mood.

Don't forget those feel-good endorphins! This brain chemical can successfully counteract the stress and negative feelings in our lives, which can certainly play a role in treating depression.

The Impact of Not Smiling

For some, the greatest motivation to try something new is to realize how much damage they can do if they do not change. Author Mark Jewell writes in the article "Shop 'Til You Smile"[48] that people who are down and sad tend to be a bit self-absorbed, which leads to spending more money.

He explains:

People's spending judgment goes out the window when they're down, especially if they're a bit self-absorbed. A recent study— study participants who watched a sadness-inducing video clip offered to pay nearly four times as much money to buy a water bottle than a group that watched an emotionally neutral clip. This is the so-called "misery is not miserly" phenomenon that is well-known to psychologists, advertisers and personal shoppers alike...

...The researcher concluded sadness can trigger a chain of emotions leading to extravagant tendencies. Sadness leads people to become more focused on themselves, causing the person to feel that they and their possessions are worth little. That feeling increases willingness to pay more – presumably to feel better about themselves.

While spending money, especially if it isn't readily available, can be problematic for those who are unhappy in life, there are many other ways in which not smiling can decrease quality of life and lead to increased relationship problems.

Consider your own friends and family. Who do you enjoy being around the most? Those who are smiling and happy, or those who are depressed, angry and always seem to have a negative outlook?

It's easy to understand how not smiling can isolate an individual and create even more disappointment and hardship.

The good news is that even when times are difficult, even when we do not feel like it, there is transformational power in the act of smiling. The physical turning-up the corners of our mouths into a grin or teeth-baring smile will get the endorphins flowing into the bloodstream, leading to a boost in mood that money can't buy.

We can change our lives and the lives of those around us by making the choice to smile through life. While many things are out of our control, a smile is something we are always capable of doing to make a positive impact.

Try these next few smile tips out:

It's All about Attitude

One specific study that Christopher Peterson, Ph. D[49] has had on going at the University of Michigan found the direct link between an optimistic smile and health. He says optimistic people create a different biological makeup that boosts their immune system. The right attitude in life keeps you open to healthy ideas and overall health means more smiles.

Smile Yourself Silly

Practicing your smile might seem obsessive, even narcissistic, but remember those endorphins. Just like exercise releases endorphins, you can get a good boost by smiling 50 times right in row. Do that in mirror every morning and you'll be sure to start the day laughing at your funny face.

The Bigger the Better

Smiling wider than a grin enhances the pleasure derived from the act. On simple experiment used by some psychologists is to hold a pen horizontal between the teeth and grin as wide as possible, then repeat the grin with the pen placed horizontal between the lips in front of the teeth. Notice how much better a wide, unrestrained smile feels and remember that the next time you restrain the natural state of a smile into a grin; don't hold back.

Get Out of Jail Free

While a smile may seem highly inappropriate when you're on trial by jury, a phenomenon known as the Smile-Leniency Effect shows that judges give smilers lighter penalties. Several court studies revealed this and even when guilty as charged, a smile softens the edges of even the hardest criminal. While we trust you aren't facing a trail but try this next time you get pulled over by a policeman.

A Defensive Smile

Smiling is often an immediate reaction that accompanies embarrassment and rightly so. A smile or laugh can ease away the tension of an embarrassing moment and may be the brain's defense against the influx of stress from blushing cheeks.

A Smile and Your Spiritual Life

According to the article *Social Smile – An Interesting Comparison*[50] one of the first positive signs in a normal Christian is an acknowledgement of Christ—the spiritual smile. The author explains that the spiritual smile is similar to the social smile, and it is one of the earliest milestones a Christian reaches. We can look to the Bible to see the value God places on smiles and laughter:

- Psalm 2:4:"The One enthroned in heaven, laughs!"

- Proverbs 17:22: "A cheerful heart is good medicine, but a downcast spirit dries up the bones!"

- 1 John 1:4: "These things we write, so that our joy may be made complete."

Smile Stories… Healing from Tragedy

On December 19, 2006, my mom, my dad, and my older brother were all killed in a car accident. They were driving from Iowa to Colorado to spend Christmas with me. I was 20 years old. They hit a patch of black ice, slid into the oncoming lane, and were hit head-on by a semi truck.

I spent Christmas alone. My boyfriend was in California with his family. When he came back he kept trying to cheer me up but never could. I was so depressed for so long. I never wanted to go out or hang with friends. All I wanted to do was sit at home and watch TV.

On January 3, 2007, my boyfriend, the love of my life, broke up with me. I stopped eating. I stopped drinking. I stopped sleeping. Every time I ate or drank something, it was tasteless. Every time I slept, I would wake up crying from the nightmares I had about my family dying.

I only weighed 107 pounds when they died. Three weeks after it happened, I had lost 40 pounds total. I looked like a Holocaust victim. After one solid week, a full seven days, with no sleep, no naps, no dozing, I started hallucinating. Everywhere I looked, I saw my family. My dad was a taxi driver. My mom was a gas station cashier. My brother was on the elevator in my apartment building. I didn't see them as I remembered them, though. I saw them covered in blood with torn clothes and tears running down their faces. They all said the same thing to me, "This is all your fault. You should've stayed in Iowa."

I couldn't take it anymore. It was time to end it. I missed them so much. I had to be with them. I went to Wal-Mart and bought some Play Dough to clog up my tail pipe with. I decided that I was going to drive out to a rarely traveled back road so there would be less of a chance that someone would find me and save me just in time.

I was at a stop light on my way out of the city, when I looked at the car next to me. There was a family inside having a wonderful time. In the back passenger seat was a little girl who couldn't have been more than five years old. She looked back at me, smiled, and waved. I smiled and waved back.

The light turned green and I didn't notice until the car that the girl was in started pulling forward. I looked at the license plate and it said: DNTGIVUP. Don't give up. It was an Iowa plate from the same county that I grew up in, where my family was coming from. I couldn't do it.

My family wouldn't have wanted me to give up. I turned around and went home. When I got there, there was a message on my answering machine from my boyfriend wanting to get back together. To this day, I don't know if the little girl or the license plate made more of an impact. But I do know that if that little girl hadn't smiled at me, I wouldn't have looked at the license plate, and I would be with my family right now.

So keep smiling. You never know when you might save a life.

Smile Stories… The Joy of Surprise

If my eyes meet someone else's I often smile at them, I smile because I think why not, life is hard enough on all of us. What I enjoy most about smiling at strangers is that when they look surprised it makes me want to laugh really hard but I feel

I have to control the laughter in this case and not just burst out so I just smile more widely and look away and chuckle to myself quietly once the urgency of the laugh eases. Some people actually scowl back and when they do I usually can't conceal the laugh with a smile, I just laugh outright. When they smile back at me it makes me feel good. It's a win-win, I don't think I have ever smiled at anyone and not walked away smiling myself either because they smiled back or because I was laughing at their reaction.

I think I have run into people who were doing the same thing to me that I do to other people, see I never expect anyone to smile at me first so it's always a surprise.

Next

The psychological aspects of smiling are amazing. Next we'll look at how smiling affects us physically.

Chapter 5:

How Smiling Makes You Healthier

Always keep your smile. That's how I explain my long life.
Jeanne Calment
Longest confirmed lifespan, 122 years, 164 days

In a society that seems to be focused on youthfulness and increasing longevity of life, it is of great value to consider how **a simple smile can improve health and add years to life**. In contrast, it's safe to say that the negative emotions we allow to take over our lives and show on our faces can lead to health problems and an earlier death. What if rather than or in addition to seeking out expensive medications and therapies, we took advantage of the healing power of a smile?

In *Smile! The Secret Science of Smiling,*[51] Star writes that there is research suggesting that a smile is "an inoculation of energy that ignites an enduring sense of buoyancy and well-being and fuels the ongoing perception that life is fulfilling, pleasant and meaningful".

When we choose to smile and consciously activate positive emotions, our heart's field electromagnetically transmits to our environment, which goes to show why smiling can be contagious and make people around you smile in return.

He references a study conducted in the 1930s, observing nuns who wrote personal essays about their lives. The study revealed that the nuns who wrote biographies reflecting positive emotional content lived up to 10 years longer and had fewer diagnoses of dementia.

The researcher explained this phenomenon by illustrating that electromagnetic field generated by the heart is at the center of this process. Star writes that today's research is showing that our heart's field is registered physiologically and it has the potential to influence the brain activities of those around us.

When we choose to smile and consciously activate positive emotions, our heart's field electromagnetically transmits to our environment, which goes to show why smiling can be contagious and make people around you smile in return.

Remember: It's the genuine smile that is not only on your face, but from your heart, that can create this positive energy flow that leads to increased health and happiness. However, there is still room for the "fake it 'til you make it" method. According to Star, research shows that when you fake a smile, stand up straight, keep your chin-up and inhale deeply, it is nearly impossible to remain in a depressive state for that moment.

In this way, you can force yourself to create the positive emotion in your heart's electromagnetic field by putting a smile on your face.

It has been said that animals, and even plants, respond to these electromagnetic signals. They are powerful and can be transformational for not only ourselves but for those with whom we come in contact.

Patch Adams Quotes: The Healing Power of Smiles and Laughter

- "The more we spread the word about our work, the more we help others rethink the system, the more powerful that revolution will be."

- "Remember laughing? Laughter enhances the blood flow to the body's extremities and improves cardiovascular function. Laughter releases endorphins and other natural mood elevating and pain-killing chemicals, improves the transfer of oxygen and nutrients to internal organs.
  Laughter boosts the immune system and helps the body fight off disease, cancer cells as well as viral, bacterial and other infections. Being happy is the best cure of all diseases!"

- "Health is based on happiness-from hugging and clowning around to finding joy in family and friends…."

(Source: www.patchadamsspeaks.com)

What is Psychoneuroimmunology?

A technique in which healthcare professionals use humor, smiling and laughter to help patients cope with pain and illness this mouthful of a word "psychoneuroimmunology" provides for us a study of how the mind and behaviors affect health and the ability to ward off as well as heal from disease.

Health care professionals throughout the U.S. have started utilizing these "humor" techniques and are achieving powerful results. They are proving what we have believed to be true in our own research and life experiences: smiling promotes good health.

One impressive example of psychoneuroimmunology is the story of Dr. Norman cousins who cured himself of bone cancer and other diseases through laughter. In his book, Star shares the doctor's story of how he began watching funny movies and constantly laughing and smiling, which in turn elevated his endorphins and other immune system healers including T-cells, lymphocytes, leucocytes and phagocytes—each of these work to fight disease.

A more famous example is Patch Adams—the man after whom the "Patch Adams" movie starring Robin Williams was made. Adams is a medical doctor, humanitarian clown, and social change activist, who uses humor to promote healing, particularly in children facing diseases.

Adams explains his philosophy:

I have reached the conclusion that humor is vital in healing the problems of individuals, communities and societies. I have tried to make my own life silly, not as that word is currently used, but in terms of its original meaning. "Silly" originally meant good, happy, blessed, fortunate, kind and cheerful in many different languages. No other attribute has been more important. Wearing a rubber nose wherever I go has changed my life. Dullness and boredom melt away. Humor has made my life joyous and fun. It can do the same for you. Wearing underwear on the outside of your clothes can turn a tedious trip to the store for a forgotten carton of milk into an amusement park romp. People so unabashedly thank you for entertaining them[52].

It is interesting to see how in using humor and smiling to help others, it has resulted in a more fulfilling and joyous life for Dr. Adams, because he spends a significant amount of his time smiling, laughing and "clowning-around." The health benefits of psychoneuroimmunology are contagious—passing between people and infiltrating the electromagnet fields of our hearts into our environments and the people around us.

A cheerful heart is good medicine,
but a crushed spirit dries up the bones.

– Proverbs 17:22

How to Practice the "Healing Smile[53]"

Practicing an "Internal Smile" can be great therapeutic practice to work through stress or bring healing, according to Daniel Reinaldo Bernstein, L.Ac., CH.

This "Inner Smile" method leads to eliminating pain-based syndromes of all kinds, including arthritis, myofascial pain, frozen shoulder, as well as anxiety, depression and digestive problems.

- We begin by closing our eyes and smiling directly into our eyes. Simply relax and feel a deep, warm smile shine in and through your eyes. We are relaxing the sympathetic and the parasympathetic nervous systems. The sympathetic nervous system controls our fight-or-flight response—it's our gas pedal—while the parasympathetic deals with 'rest and digest', and is the 'brake.' Since these two systems are linked to every organ and gland in the body, being able to control these functions has far reaching implications for the health of any individual.

- Experience your eyes tingling with the Inner Smile.

- Direct that energy to fill your internal organs with the same healing energy, the love that you've brought up to your eyes from your spirit. Organize the pathway into 3 separate directions:

1. The Front Path: Smile down into the eyes, face, throat, heart, lungs, liver and genital area

2. The Middle Path: Smile down and direct the energy via your saliva to your stomach, small intestine, colon and rectum

3. The Back Path: Smile down your vertebrae of your spine, one by one.

Source: http://bluephoenixwellness.com/the-healing-smile-and-how-to-use-it/

The Power of Smiles in a Hospital Setting

Author Star in Smile! The Secret Science of Smiling addresses how many contemporary hospitals have special areas with televisions showing comedy programs or old movies on funny subjects to promote smiling from patients who may be without smiles and facing despair and discouragement.

...by smiling, you actually change the pattern of information going from your body to your brain. This has a big impact on health and well-being—both short-term and long-term, states Dr. McCraty (p.104).

– Elan Sun Star, Smile! The Secret Science of Smiling

Much like Patch Adams' methods, these hospitals encourage physicians and counselors to dress as clowns, distribute comic books, games and toys to increase rapport and motivate patients to participate more actively in their treatments[54].

Even if the patients are not feeling happiness with their emotions and minds, the act of smiling itself works to create a state of happiness, which brings us back to the ideas surrounding the "fake it 'til you make it" approach.

Science has revealed that by "consciously cultivating a smile—both on your face and in your heart—you can take a proactive role in creating your own health, happiness, and fulfillment, while positively affecting others and your environment[55].

Years ago the Humor Project sponsored the creation of Humor Carts or Comedy carts for hospitals. They were so effective at helping in the healing process there are now well over 8,000 of them in hospitals today. Smiling helps in the healing process.

How Smiling Affects Well-Being and Quality of Life

Having a smile on one's face will bring with it an increased well-being and quality of life as it increases those positive-emotion parts of the brain and sends a message to others around us, who then return the smile. Imagine going through life without smiling at others or without people smiling at you.

Whether we are walking down the street, at church, or in our own homes, we crave that type of positive affirmation that can only come from a smile someone gives to us.

It's interesting to note that studies have shown people who have facial defects or are unable to smile have significantly decreased quality of life. A study from 1995 from researchers Gift and Atchinson[56] showed that these patients in the study had diseases and disorders that resulted in dental and craniofacial defects that thwarted their quality of life, disturbing self-image, self-esteem and well-being. These patients lived a poorer quality of life and had a tendency to avoid social contact, all because of their inability to show a healthy smile.

Smiling and Mental Health[57]

Dr. Cliff Kuhn, M.D., also known as "The Laugh Doctor" shares how smiling can make a big difference in mental health:

"The first Fun Commandment I recommend for improved mental health is "Always Go the Extra Smile." This Commandment is doubly helpful for depression and anxiety, because not only does it provide measurable emotional and physical relief, but it also is completely under your control—regardless of your circumstances....It can be you greatest resource for using humor's natural medicine to accelerate your mental health.

Smiling produces measurable physical benefits you can experience immediately: your stress decreases, your immunity improves, your pain and frustration tolerances increase, and your creativity soars..."

Source: Kuhn, C. (n.d.). Natural Medicine of Humor Adds Happiness to Your Life Right Away.natural-humor-medicine. com. Retrieved January 21, 2013, from http://www.natural-humor-medicine.com/

How can this relate to us in our daily lives? Although we may not have disfigurement or defects that prevent our smiling, life circumstances can leave us without positive expressions on our faces.

We allow the outside world to control our facial expressions and, whether we are aware of this or not, the lack of smiling can directly impact the enjoyment we get out of life and the people around us.

Often, when we have a tendency toward negative facial expressions—a frown or a scowl—we may not even be aware of how often we are scrunching up our faces in an unpleasant way.

Spend a day being as aware as you can be of what you are doing with your face. In the car, at work, prepping dinner at home, spending time with family members—during each of these activities make yourself consciously aware of your face.

You may be surprised by how often you are scowling throughout the day, and this can absolutely impact the quality of your day. When you feel your face in a scowl or with brows furrowed, spend a few moments to turn-around your facial express, and you might just turn around your entire day.

Ready to turn that frown upside down?

Here's what you can do:

1. Feel your face in a scowl, frown, glare, or other negative facial expression.

2. Immediately stop what you are doing, pause for a moment and focus on relaxing those tense facial muscles.

3. Take a deep breath in and release, and as you exhale the hair, release the muscle tension.

4. Then, whether you feel like it or not, put your face into the "smile position"—turn up the corners of your mouth, bear your teeth and go for it.

5. You should immediately feel a release of tension, and improved day is likely to follow.

In her article "The Smile Effect," Author Veronika Bulochova discusses research for "pose smiling" or faking a smile to get a positive physiological response:

> *The research on "Power Posing" by D. R. Carney includes the evidence from other studies: "In research on embodied cognition, some evidence suggests that bodily movements, such as facial displays, can effect emotional states. For example, unobtrusive contraction of the "smile muscle" (i.e. the zygomaticus major) increases enjoyment[58]". Though the research by Carney has been focused on a wide variety of posing (nodding, posture and other) it also included a pose-smiling (a non-Duchenne smile) in a high-power display. The results proved to be consistent with the hypotheses and show the occurrence of physiological changes and relevant feelings as an effect of posing. As it can be seen, smiling has been observed to make us feel good…[59]*

Smiling Leads to a Long Life

If smiling helps with healing, immune function and improved outlook on life, it makes sense that it also contributes to longevity. But what does science say about this?

In her article "Does Smiling Lead to Longevity and Perceptions of Attractiveness," Nivea Ferreira Schut[60] discusses research published in Psychological Science regarding intensity of smiles and longer life.

By analyzing photos and statistical information of the Major League Baseball players, researchers Abel and Kruger investigated whether a relation exists between the intensity of smiles on players' photos and how long they lived.

According the original article titled "Smile Intensity in Photographs Predicts Longevity,[61]" the results of the study showed that on average, players with a full smile lived the longest, followed by players with partial smiles. Those who lived shorter lives were the players who had no smile in their photographs.

Abel and Kruger explained: "…individuals whose underlying emotional disposition is reflected in voluntary or involuntary Duchenne smiles may be basically happier than those with less intense smiles, and hence more predisposed to benefit from the effects of positive emotionality."

In other words, a smile on one's face in general reveals a happier life, increased well-being and leads to a longer life. http://www.youtube.com/watch?v=oC0qRrT2EtE[62]

Smiling for Health Longevity of Life Video Resources

- Smile—the Secret to Longevity for 95-year-old: http://www.youtube.com/watch?v=oC0qRrT2EtE

- The Contagious Smile: http://www.youtube.com/watch?v=fHQBghevMLw&feature=related[63]

- Practicing the Inner Smile: http://www.youtube.com/watch?v=ML5uQAHQHVs&feature=related[64]

- Smile—the Predictor of a Long Life: http://www.youtube.com/watch?v=U9cGdRNMdQQ

- Face Yoga for the Perfect Smile: http://www.youtube.com/watch?v=r_0a63QQroE&feature=related[65]

Healthy Smile: An Indicator of Good Health

In addition to increasing quality of life and increasing positive physiological responses, a healthy smile can also tell us something about the person. Research has shown that healthy smiles can actually be an indicator of good health.

When we discuss "healthy smiles," we are referencing not only the physical action of smiling, but also the health and appearance of the teeth, gums and mouth involved in the smiling. Good dental care has a big impact on overall health and lack of care can lead to accelerated tooth decay and gum disease, which can in turn lead to even more severe health issues.

The diseases and health issues resulting from poor dental care include cardiovascular disease, diabetes, pregnancy and birth complications and cancer. On the other hand, good dental hygiene is likely to exist in people who have better overall health.

An oral health article on HealthyPeople.gov[66] references studies that have shown that women with periodontal disease were more likely to have low birth weight or premature babies than women who have healthy gums. This same article explains a relationship between periodontal disease and heart disease, which may be due to the type of bacteria that grows in the mouth, producing the same type of chemicals that cause inflammation in the cardiovascular system.

Other connections between poor dental care and health:

- Increased risk for heart disease, hearth attacks and strokes
- In the elderly, those with poor oral health were more likely to get pneumonia, as bacteria in the mouth made its way into the lungs.

Smiling and the Health-Conscious Person

Whether you have always been concerned about maximizing your health, or are trying to turn-over a new leaf to achieve your optimal level of health, smiling is a free, all-natural method to boosting immunity, preventing disease as well as healing from disease and illness.

In our modern society, we are quick to turn to the latest medication for a quick-fix without the effort, but by putting forth a little effort to smile more in our day, we will experience greater effects for less cost and with no dangerous side-effects.

Even better, you do not need to wait until your next doctor's appointment or until you can get a prescription. No waiting in doctor's offices. No waiting in lines at the drugstore. Just smile.

The power is in your hands today, in this very moment. This doesn't mean you must suddenly plaster a fake smile on your face everywhere you go. Rather, you can begin to increase self-awareness of the facial expressions you make throughout your day and make an effort to decrease those times of scowling and frowning by pausing, inhaling, exhaling, releasing facial tension and turning your mouth into a relaxed smile.

This little effort can create big results in your life. The simple act of smiling will decrease tension and stress, which will create a positive flow of energy from you to your environment and those around you. It literally creates a ripple-effect of positivity that can only improve your relationships, as you are simultaneously improving your health and overall well-being.

It may sound cliché, but we truly only have one life to live. Smiling enables us to make the most of the time we have on earth—enriching our own lives and the lives of those who come in contact with us.

Endless Medication

Smiling and laughing are intimately connected and both use muscles that never really tire. While you may have laughed so hard your face hurt, it's guaranteed that when the laugh fest is over, there will still be a smile on your face. Overall, there is no downside to smiling and you can't ever smile too much, just at the wrong time.

Chin Up

When we keep our heads up, the term, 'keep your chin up' has real physiological benefits. Notice that when you stretch your neck backward and look up, a natural smile forms in the facial muscles. There are many simple movements in the practice of yoga that produce this effect and probably why everyone has a giant grin on their face after a yoga session.

A Healthy Smile

One reason to smile is to celebrate your health, but smiling itself is a ticket to better health through neurotransmitters. Numerous medical and psychological studies have found that through the triggering of certain hormones, a smile promotes good overall health. This leads to lower heart rates, steady breathing and the ability to smile through stressful situations.

It's easier than frowning

As a naturally induced movement, the recognition of joy or pleasure involuntarily triggers smiles. It takes more muscles and effort to frown, where a smile relieves stress, a frown or perplexed expression can induce more stress. Prove it to yourself and notice that facial muscles relax in a smile, allowing blood to flow freely through vessels. The contortion of a frown exhausts the facial muscles, a clear warning from the brain that you need to relax.

Smile Stories… Support at the Right Time

I have had to face many difficult problems in my life. My biggest challenges were concerning my health. In the time I've been married, I've been admitted to the hospital several times. First, for the removal of uterine fibroids. I was so tense and anxious. Being uncomfortable discussing my problems with others didn't make adjusting any easier. I did what I usually do – suffer alone. I was worried about whether I could ever have children after this surgery. My husband was very supportive but I couldn't know his inner feelings. My state of anxiety led us to fighting frequently.

At last, the day of the surgery arrived. I was lying on the hospital bed and suddenly a nurse came to my room. She was an older nurse, the head of the nursing department there. She started talking, and I was put so at ease as she spoke that I could feel myself gaining strength to meet the challenges of surgery.

She was great. As we spoke, she explained the difficulties I would face after the surgery. She gave me a pleasant smile whenever she looked at me. She asked me to be courageous and told me that all my relatives and parents waiting outside needed to be consoled at this time. She said, "I know that you are tense. But just give support for your parents who are tense. Just smile and it will be the greatest thing which you should do before the surgery."

I suddenly became alert and started thinking of my mother. That courage enabled me to talk with my family. I think of that nurse and how her smile and compassion gave me strength.

We've seen how smiling can help us feel better and even make us live longer. Now let's look at the different kinds of smiles and what they communicate.

Smile Stories... Smile Wins the Job and More

When I was a kid, my parents taught me that it was very important to smile, and that I was a beautiful little girl with a beautiful smile. At that time, I didn't believe them. Later in life I now understand the meaning of their words.

My first job ever was as a hotel receptionist. The director was supposed to choose between me and another girl who had also applied for the job. He chose me because I had a beautiful smile, he said. From then on, I was always smiling, no matter how hard it was.

One day my future husband spotted me on a bus. He got close to me and said, "Hello smiley!" He taught me to be more extroverted instead of being so shy. He taught me everything I know and what I am. Now that I'm 22, I'm still always smiling, and I'm still working as hotel receptionist.

Smile Stories... Smile Beats Depression

I am a 20 year old woman from the United States. I am currently a student, but work part-time as a clerk at a clothing store. I am single, but have been dating for several years now. Furthermore, I am a bit of both an extrovert and an introvert.

When I first meet people, I tend to be shy and keep to myself. However, around my group of friends and coworkers,

I tend to be loud and carefree. Being a happy go lucky person that tends to enjoy time with family and friends has shaped my attitude.

While I was not always this bubbly and fun loving person, smiling has changed my outlook on life and even my health. I have been suffering chronic depression for years now, but it is a battle I have been winning. Smiling is a key reason for this. Not only does smiling change your outlook on the day, but it changes how others perceive you. As a result, the depression becomes lessened, and it is easier to get through the day. Furthermore, it has been proven that smiling releases natural pain killers that not only ease the pain of depression, but brighten your mood. Finally, smiling works muscles in the face that relieve stress and improve your overall health.

Smile Stories... Smiling Revives a Life

I went through a very dark period in my life after making the discovery that sent my life into a spiral, my wife sleeping with another man. I really didn't think I was capable of smiling again, for months I was in a hole of anger and depression. My health even started to decline and I started to experience symptoms I had never experienced before, mostly in my heart and I'm sure contributed by anxiety.

It was a very hard thing to do but I actually started to force myself to smile, find any reason to do so. Eventually, by pretending to smile, I actually did start smiling. Things started to become positive little by little. I got the divorce and honestly lost my feelings for her quicker than I thought I would.

I was standing on the green field looking back at the side of life with dying grass. The more I smiled, the more I laughed, the better my health got. I have since moved on and found someone who is kind and honest and who makes me smile on a daily basis. Life is good, so there is no reason not to smile.

Next

We've seen how smiling can help us feel better and even make us live longer. Now let's look at the different kinds of smiles and what they communicate.

Chapter 6:

Different Smiles for Different Occasions

A smile appeared upon her face as if she'd taken it directly from her handbag and pinned it there.
— **Loma Chandler,** Author

Each person has many different types of smiles to express a wide range of emotions. We rarely stop to consider what our smiles mean and the messages they send to others, or whether it is appropriate or inappropriate for a particular setting. Let's pause to think about it now.

When you smile:

- How do others perceive you?

- What do you want to communicate when you are smiling back at someone?

- Do you understand how different smiles are better and more effective for certain situations?

- Do you know how to utilize one of your many different smiles to achieve the desired results?

It is very important to grasp the significance of your smile. How you use it plays a major role in how you relate to people in your life. In all of our research on smiling, the information provided by Paul

Ekman, author of *Emotions Revealed: Recognizing Faces and Feelings to Improve Communication and Emotional Life*[67] and *Telling Lies*[68], regarding the classifications of different types of smiles seemed to provide the most thorough research on the subject. We will discuss Ekman's research in this chapter in order to help you gain a better understanding of the different smile types you possess and how you can use these types to your advantage in your life.

If you have gone through life thus far primarily unaware of the types of smile you use in different scenarios, it is safe to say that you can take this information and begin to use these smiles more efficiently to create the social results you desire—whether that be in attracting a new love relationship, relating to family members better, or increasing your chances for success in the workplace.

Ekman's Categories of Smiles

Enjoyment Smile

One of Ekman's primary categories of smiles was the "enjoyment smile." An interesting aspect of the enjoyment smile is that it shares commonalities with other smiles in this category. For example, the enjoyment smile shares the Duchenne marker with other smiles.

As we've covered, this is when the eye squints, as you can see in any natural smile expression. Smiles featuring the Duchenne marker are associated with positive emotion, and they are typically genuine, uncontrolled smiles, meaning they just happen; they are not typically forced.

People who receive these enjoyment smiles can sense the genuineness, because the smile takes over the face—the eyes and the mouth. In contrast, a fake smile may just be smiling with the mouth, while the eyes are without the contraction of the eye muscles.

If you smile when no one else is around, you really mean it.
Andy Rooney

Felt Smile

A subcategory of the enjoyment smile is the "felt smile." This smile could be described as smiling only with the eyes. It takes place when the "simple action of the zygomatic major muscle produces the smile shown for genuine, uncontrolled, positive emotions," (Ekman, 2009. P. 151).

The zygomatic major is actually the muscle responsible for most of the differences between the smile types. It raises the cheek and the skin below the eye and causes the crow's feet wrinkle.

This rather expressive muscle is center stage when it comes to the felt smile. In fact, no other muscles in the lower part of the face are involved in this smile; just the tightening of the muscle that surrounds the eyes.

The felt smile typically is longer-lasting and more intense than other smiles and tends to emerge naturally when positive emotions are extreme. Ekman characterized the felt smile as one of the most genuine, natural smile responses:

I believe that all of the positive emotional experiences—enjoyment of another person, the happiness of relief, pleasure from tactile, auditory or visual stimulation, amusement, contentment—are shown by the felt smile and differ only in the timing and intensity of that action. (Ekman, 2009, p. 151)

Ekman's Categories of Smiles

- Enjoyment Smile
- Felt Smile
- Enjoyment of Others
- Happiness of Relief
- Pleasure from Tactile, Auditory or Visual Stimulation
- Amusement

Source: Ekman's books, *Emotions Revealed: Recognizing Faces and Feelings to Improve Communication and Emotional Life* and *Telling Lies*

While the enjoyment smile and felt smile are perhaps the most common genuine smiles in our smile arsenals, Ekman categorized several other types of smiles that we often use in different social and relational situations.

Also falling under the Enjoyment Smile category with the felt smile are the following subcategories:

Enjoyment of Others

This smile is often characterized as a sweet, pleasant smile; it may be used when we are simply enjoying the company of another person, or it could be a romantic "I'm in love" type smile. The recipient of the smile may be a best friend, girlfriend, boyfriend, spouse---whoever it is, this person is bringing the "smiler" happiness in the moment, so the natural response is to use the enjoyment of others smile.

Happiness of Relief

This smile comes from a place of relief—thankfulness for not having to deal with a fear, threat or worry that seemed to be looming. For example, this smile may emerge after driving by a police officer doing 85 mph in a 65 mph-zone and realizing the officer is not coming after you.

The popular movie Hunger Games provides another example—the people who were not selected to be contestants in the terrifying games often had happiness of relief smiles on their faces. This was a life and death situation, and they were obviously feeling relief in an intense way!

Pleasure from Tactile, Auditory or Visual Stimulation

Sitting in a chair, petting a soft, furry pet often brings out this kind of pleasurable smile—at least in animal lovers. The person is experiencing tactile pleasure and a natural smile results. Listening to music is another common cause of this smile.

Amusement

Perhaps one of the most common felt smiles, the amusement smile is a result of something that amuses you. It may be from a comedy routine or something as simple as a toddler playing, but you are feeling entertained and amused by what you are experiencing and the smile emerges on your face.

Contentment

A great example of the contentment smile is the expression you might see on an elderly couple who has been together for a long time and they are just happy and at peace together. There doesn't need to be anything particularly happy or humorous happening; it's just that they are genuinely content to walk through life together, and this smile is a visible result of that contentment.

In addition to the smile categories as described by Ekman, we have come up with the following smile types to break-down the categories even further:

Botox

The Botox smile is an interesting type of smile, because although the muscles around the eye are paralyzed due to a Botox procedure, the smile is still categorized as "felt." You do not see the eye squinting typical of a felt smile, therefore, it is often difficult to determine if the smile is a genuine felt smile or a fake, forced smile such as a Pan-Am smile (talked about later in this chapter).

Because of this, Botox can lead to confusion to the recipients of the smile, as they are unsure if it is a genuine smile or not. People who have received Botox treatment may find that it is difficult to communicate the desired message with their smiles, because even if they are truly feeling and displaying a felt smile, it may appear to lack realness because it is not reflected in their eyes.

Arrogant

This smile conveys a message of arrogance—someone thinking they are superior to those around them. The popular television show *Dance Moms* often provides plenty of examples of this smile type in the mothers who are parading their daughters around in dance competitions. Whether they are trying to intimidate others or just believe they are better than others, the arrogant smile pops up quite often on the faces of the dance moms.

Confident

This is an important smile in your smile repertoire, as it communicates the message of confidence and being sure about yourself. The confident smile comes across when you know you have something about which to be proud and you know you have accomplished something.

It is especially beneficial in the career world to use a confident smile to send the message that you are competent and sure that you are the best candidate for the job or promotion. The confident smile is also a good tool to use when you are in a position of leadership and need to earn the trust and respect of those people you are leading.

Laughing

It's difficult to fake a laughing smile, as it comes from a place of genuine laughter and joy. Typically the mouth is open slightly more than it is in most felt smiles and the eye muscles are very engaged.

The intensity of the laughing smile is based on the intensity of the humor you are experiencing. This smile is very contagious and often causes others to engage in the laughing smile with you, even without clever punch lines!

Sexy

This genuine smile results from a moment in which someone is striving to be attractive to another person or group of people. It is typically associated with certain positions of the body and it utilized to attract members of the opposite sex.

Models and actresses tend to have this type of smile down to a science, and it can be very powerful when using it to influence others. It not only gets attention, but enables them to get what they want.

Ekman's Subcategory of Felt Smiles—Blended with Emotions

Going back to Ekman's categories of smiles, we can see how he created a subcategory of felt smiles for the smiles that were blended with two or more emotions experienced at once but registered within the same facial expression. Let's take a look at the smiles that fall under this category:

Enjoyable-Excitement

In this type of smile, Ekman noted that the upper eyelid is raised in addition to having the characteristics of a felt smile. He provided the example of film actor Harpo Marx, who often displayed this excited, gleeful smile, often when pulling a prank. He was both excited about what he was doing and enjoying what he was doing, so the facial expressions blended to create this enjoyable-excitement felt smile.

Enjoyable-Surprised

Also characterized as a "lucky" smile, in this expression the brow is raised and the jaw dropped, while the upper lid is raised and the typical felt smile is displayed. Think of it as the "I just won the lottery" type of smile. You will see this smile when people are surprised by something positive. Often the hands will go up to the face as they display this smile.

Children at Christmas are known to have the enjoyable-surprised smile when they see what Santa Claus has left them under the tree. It's fun to see someone with this smile, and it tends to evoke smiles in others.

Enjoyable-Embarrassed

In this felt smile sub-category, the smile is slightly dampened due to the feeling of embarrassment. Often people's hands will come up over their mouths during this particular smile, because they are trying to hide something. This smile can also emerge when people are embarrassed but in an enjoyable or humorous way.

On the other hand, it can be culturally-related, as in Japan where it is common for the women to smile in this way, because it isn't always culturally-acceptable for them to show their happiness in an obvious way.

Yet another example of this smile is when people are embarrassed by their smile or their teeth, lips or gums. They may be truly enjoying themselves, but they tend to pull back at smiling, or use their hands to shield the visibility of their smile components. Perhaps they have broken or crooked teeth or overexposed gums—whatever the reason, they are feeling joyful but are not comfortable enough with their smile's appearance to reveal their mouth.

Felt Smile with a Particular Gaze

This smile contains two types, flirtatious and embarrassed:

- *Flirtatious*—this felt smile has much more than just the basic smile and often involves hand gestures as well; it may involve smiling and then gazing away flirtatiously from the person of interest, and then turning back to glance again at the person just long enough to be noticed. This is actually one of the elements of the painting of Mona Lisa, because Leonardo reportedly depicted her caught in the midst of a flirtatious smile, facing one way, and then glancing sideways at the object of her interest. The gaze shift lasts only a moment, but creates a big impact.

- *Embarrassment*—also characterized as a shy smile, in this type the gaze is directed down or to the side in such a way that the embarrassed person does not meet the other person's eyes directly. There may be a momentary upward lift of the skin and muscle between the lower lip and chin during this type of felt smile. Princess Diana's famous shy smile is a good example of this type.

Ekman's Category of Non-Enjoyment Smiles

There are times when a person smiles yet they are not feeling joy or pleasure or they *are* feeling joy, but they try to cover it up. These are the times when someone might use a non-enjoyment smile. Some examples of these include:

Dampened Smile

For this type of smile, the person may actually feel positive emotion, but they are trying to cover it up so others will not think that their emotions are as intense as they truly are. This is common in social situations in which you do not want to appear overly emotional. You want to give the appearance of being in control, such as in a business setting or very public social event.

Another common scenario for using this smile is when you are around a serious person and you do not want to seem overly gregarious; therefore, you dampen your positive emotions to seem more subdued to match the other person's personality.

In a dampened smile, Ekman explains that the lips may be pressed, the lip corners tightened, the lower lip pushed up, the lip corners pulled down, or any combination of these actions—merging with a basic smile.

Miserable Smile

According to Ekman, the miserable smile acknowledges the experience of negative emotions. It is not an attempt to conceal but rather a facial comment on being miserable. This smile is often a result of a person who is trying to grin and bear his misery and often follow a negative emotional expression of some kind. It may also result as the person is attempting to control a negative emotion, such as fear, anger or distress.

People may also use a miserable smile to let another person know that things are not going their way and they would like some compassion or sympathy. The smile itself is characterized by the lip pressing over the lower lip, pushed down by the chin muscle, the corners tighten down—similar to the dampened smile, but coming from a different place emotionally.

The primary difference between the miserable smile and the dampened smile is the absence of any evidence of the muscle around the eyes tightening. That eye muscle contraction is there with the dampened smile, because enjoyment is being experienced; however, in the miserable smile, the enjoyment is not there, so the eye muscles are relaxed.

Same Non-Felt Smiles, Different Social Functions

Still falling under the category of Ekman's Non-Felt Smiles, the following smiles are similar in their appearance and components but differ in the social functions they serve:

Qualifier Smile

This smile is common when people are attempting to take the harsh edge off of unpleasant news, such as a critical message. An example would be a boss who had to discipline an employee. She might deliver the news with a qualifier smile first to attempt to soften the message of the critique.

The qualifier smile is set deliberately with a quick brief abrupt onset. The lip corners may be tightened sometimes to get the lower lip pushed up slightly for moment. This smile is often marked with a nod of the head and with a slightly down-turned and sideways tilt to the head while the smiler looks down to the person receiving the message.

While this is common in professional situations, the qualifier smile is also common in parents disciplining their children.

Compliance Smile

This smile acknowledges that you have something to do that you would really rather not do, but you will do it anyway without protesting. When the person delivers a compliance smile, the recipient gets the impression that the smiler is not happy and is accepting some unwanted fate or assignment.

The compliance smile resembles the qualifier smile without the tilted and lowered head position. Instead, the brows may rise for a moment, and there may even be a sigh or shrug accompanying the smile.

Coordination Smile

Also known as the Pan-Am smile, for its use by flight attendant, the coordination smile is a regulation tool that is utilized in communication between two people. It is a polite, cooperative smile expressing agreement and understanding as well as acknowledgement of another person's proper performance. The smile is slight, typically asymmetrical, and the eyes tend to be relaxed. It's a common smile people use on a day-to-day basis.

Under the subcategory of the coordination smile is another type of smile called the "listener response smile." This is a smile one uses while listening to a person speaking in order to let the speaker know that he or she understands what is being said. It also communicates to the speaker that he or she does not need to repeat what they said, because the listener gets it and is acknowledging the speaker's contribution to the conversation with the listener response smile.

Each of the four smiles listed above—qualifier, compliance, coordination and listener response—may sometimes transition into or be replaced by a genuine felt smile. If the situation comes to a resolution or agreement, or if there is a common ground between the two people communicating, it is likely that the smile will progress to a true felt smile.

False Smile

A false smile is often used when someone is attempting to convince another person that they are feeling a positive emotion when they truly are not. It may be that there is a lack of emotion or a negative emotion and the "smiler" is trying to conceal or cover up his or her true feelings, using the false smile like a mask.

The smile differs from the miserable smile in that it is misleading. The false smile also tends to be more asymmetrical than felt smiles and it is not accompanied by the eye muscle contractions. Furthermore, the false smile will not feature raised cheeks, the crow's feet wrinkles or the lowering of the eyebrow that appears in felt smiles.

A good give-away for a fake smile is when the smile starts and stops quickly. For example, someone pops on a smile when someone walks in the room and then immediately drops the smile when the person leaves. It's almost as if the smile is like a light switch, the smiler turns off and on; in other words, it's not coming from a true place of joy or happiness. It's put-on for a purpose.

Smile Stories… Hiding the Pain

At work I always have a smile on my face and it is just second nature now. However bad I feel, I am still always smiling.

www.SmilingSuccess.com/2freegifts

Because of this, people think I am very happy, which is a total lie. It's such a lie, it's ridiculous. Even today when I have felt really sad inside, I have been joking around with coworkers and acting as though nothing is wrong even when everything is.

I have so many repressed feelings and it has become normal for me to hide them all, which is not healthy but it's what I have been doing for a long time.

I come out of work and I just feel empty. Every time I come out of work, I long for someone genuinely caring to come up and look after me a bit. How pathetic is that? I just want to be looked after and treated as though I am important. I want to be held and I want to tell someone all my secrets and all my hidden pain. Will that ever happen?

Why Understanding Smile Types is Important

Going through the smile types though this chapter can help you to gain a better understanding of what different smiles mean and the messages you communicate with them. This knowledge will benefit you as you become more aware of the messages you send with your facial expressions, but it can also help you to become more in-tune with the expressions and various communications styles of those around you.

Whether you want to work on developing the proper felt smile in the right social setting or the most influential confident smile to boost your image in the business world, understanding the components of these different smile types can help you to optimize the smile messages you send on a day-to-day basis.

Remember, the most powerful smile is one that is congruent with what you are feeling and with the message you want to communicate. It can sometimes be a challenge to achieve that congruency of expression and emotion in which you are showing through your smile what you feel on the inside. But the more congruent you can be, the more people will view you as genuine and authentic, which will lead to success in a variety of different relationships and life experiences.

Can you identify the smile types in the following stories?

Smile Stories… Smiling for a Stage Mom

My husband and I judged a pageant together shortly after we married. When we arrived at the hotel, we witnessed a mother and her eleven-year-old daughter arguing because the pageant was on a Saturday and the young girl wanted to go to a birthday party…

The pageant started and the girl and her mother stood in line at the edge of the stage, waiting for the girl's turn to model for us. The girl looked so pretty and her mother kept saying to her, "Smile at the judges!"

She walked gracefully in front of all six of us judges—and as soon as her back was turned to her mother—she stuck out her tongue to the judges. The minute she turned around where her mother would see her, she was smiling again.

Her mother was standing in the wings, smiling proudly as she watched her daughter and she never knew that her advice "Smile for the judges" was defiantly disobeyed. The girl simply did not want to be there—and she could not force a smile!

So a smile can be deceptive—which the girl used with her mother to make her think she was following her advice. But it also revealed that the inner truth behind a smile will eventually come out in other ways.

Smile Stories... Smiling with My Eyes

If a smile is not on my lips, it's the twinkle in my eye. Yes, I said twinkle, and no, I don't drip of fairy dust. When I catch someone's eye on the street, eight out of ten times, I get a smile in return. I like to think that the two who didn't respond to me would still have a better day because of a nice gesture.

Sometimes though, if I'm caught up in my own thoughts and someone smiles at me, by the time I register that face and react, they've already gone by....so the person after them gets the smile!

It's crazy how a stranger just being pleasant and courteous can make you feel good inside!

Smile Stories... A Bitter End

I am a divorced woman. I separated from my husband three years back. When my husband left me I felt helpless. I was financially and emotionally broken. I had very little means to support my daughter. My ex-husband was rich and powerful. He refused to give me financial support. I started working so I could take care of her. I also started school, but had a very hard time focusing on my studies.

It was a difficult time for me. One day I was waiting for the bus. While I was standing at the bus stop, my ex-husband passed by me in his car. After looking at me, he reversed his car, stopped by my side and looked at me with smile on his face and hatred for me in his eyes. He stayed there for a while and then drove his car away. I felt as if he was telling me how miserable he had made my life.

I could not forget the look in his eyes. This was a moment I can never forget. It changed my life completely and I decided that day that I would be successful in my life. This time I meant business, and was determined to work hard. Every day I reminded myself of that smile. Now I am a successful person and have everything going for me. It is all because of that incident on the bus stop. Thank you my dear ex-husband if you would not have smiled so cruelly at me, I would not have been so successful in my life.

Next

We've just explored the different types of smiles. Now let's look at the nitty gritty details of a smile.

Chapter 7:
What Makes Up a Smile?

A smile is a curve that sets everything straight.
– **Phyllis Diller**, American Actress and Comedian

A smile is an inexpensive way to change your looks.
– **Charles Gordy**

*The expression one wears on one's face is far more important
than the clothes one wears on one's back.*
– **Dale Carnegie**, Salesman and Writer

In a recent American Academy of Periodontology poll of 253 consumers found that **50% of the respondents considered the smile the first facial feature that they notice. In this poll, 80% of people who were not happy with their smile said they were seven times more likely to have smile enhancement procedures than facelifts**. The reason is simple: the smile has the ability to send a powerful message to those around us; even *without* considering the scientific research that backs this up, people realize the smile greatly impacts one's impression to the world.

So what are the components of the smile that work together to create this all-important impression? Teeth are the obvious answer, but gums and lips also play an important role worth considering as you strive to make the most of your smile.

When all components of your smile are optimized, they can work together to give you your best possible smile, helping you to better communicate with others and send the message you want to send to the people in your life—from family members and co-workers to potential bosses and love interests.

Unlike other forms of facial enhancement, improving one's smile is often more affordable and can even be covered by many dental insurance plans. And the return on investment for such procedures can be significant, whether you are seeking monetary return through a job promotion, or emotional return through a new relationship or better communication skills.

In order to achieve a full understanding of the different components of the smile and the impact of each component, let's break down the smile and address the potential problems and available solutions.

Teeth: What Do They Contribute to Your Smile?

One of the single most important aspects of the smile is the teeth. We may not often consider our teeth as major communication tools, but when you stop to consider how they are the primary focus of the smile, it's easy to see how the teeth are actually responsible for communicating messages to those we encounter. The appearance of our teeth sends a message regarding age, gender, and personality characteristics, such as aggressiveness, intelligence and even sexiness.

Some may identify a woman with a gap between her front two teeth as having a sexy smile; however, for a man to have that same gap, it sends the message of being more "country" or less educated. In this way, the message teeth send depends upon the individual, and specifically the gender of the individual.

- 76% of people don't feel confident enough to smile in a photograph.
- 48% of people make judgments about people by the look of their smile.
- 77% of people think a smile helps psychologically
- 67% of people think smiles help romantically.

Source: http://www.londonsmiling.com/Smile_Makeover

Another aspect of teeth that impacts the message regarding age includes the length and shape of the top front teeth (central incisors):

Are they worn?

Are they flat?

If so, this may give you an older appearance.

Are they longer?

Do they have rounded edges?

If so, that tends to give a more youthful appearance.

Chances are, you haven't really considered your teeth, especially your specific central incisors, but by giving the proper attention to this aspect of your smile and taking the necessary steps to enhance your smile through the right dental care, can help you to maximize your appearance in a natural-looking way.

Cosmetic Dentist Denise Fundora of Fundora Dental in Beverly Hills, CA, explains that "changing the size and shape of your teeth can significantly improve your smile as well as rejuvenate your overall appearance. Some of my patients say that a smile make-over is better than botox in restoring a youthful appearance[69]".

How Teeth Communicate Gender and Personality

From how square or round your teeth are, to how tilted or straight your lateral incisors are, your teeth give you a more masculine or feminine smile. More than just male or female, the messages your teeth shape and alignment send about gender and personality traits can impact how people perceive you. Whether accurate or not, your smile is constantly giving non-verbal cues about your personality.

Read more on what your teeth's placement, shape, and alignment communicate about you in Chapter 3.

How Teeth Can Complement or Clash with Your Facial Shape

In addition to certain teeth having an impact on how your smile communicates your gender, age and personality, your teeth can either complement or clash with your facial shape which impacts the attractiveness of your overall appearance.[70]

For example, if you have a round face and your teeth are flat, the face can appear much wider than it is. Long teeth can emphasize a long face, while square-shaped teeth emphasize a square face, creating a less than ideal facial appearance.

In "Smile for Your face Shape"[71] author Lauren Fritsky explains that creating your optimal smile should depend upon the shape of your face, much like you select a certain hairstyle based on your facial shape:

Those with longer, or more vertical, faces look better with smiles that accentuate the horizontal aspect of their teeth. The opposite is true for rounder faces: A longer-looking grin will balance out facial wideness. A wider smile will help a square face to appear more oval and balance out a heart-shaped mug.

Other tips for cosmetic dental work to achieve your ideal smile include:

- Those with smaller faces should avoid long or square teeth, because they can appear too dominant and disproportioned.

- Someone with a fuller face-shape should consider longer teeth as they lead to a slimming effect.

- Someone with a thinner face should avoid long or thin teeth that can lengthen the face; instead, choose wider teeth to create a fuller-face effect.

- Those with square-shaped faces should seek methods for softening the edges of sharper teeth, which will lead to a softer overall look.

How Tooth Length Impacts the Smile

In your quest to achieve your ideal smile, you may find that porcelain veneers or crowns are a good option, but you will need to work with your dentist to determine the best tooth length for your appearance.

Porcelain veneers and crowns can be shortened or lengthened to create the right look for an individual patient. Your dentist should be able to assist you through this process and help you to analyze what length you should choose to enhance your smile and facial shape.

Dr. Norman Huefner, cosmetic dentist in Orange County, CA, explains on his website[72] some of the ways in which the length of teeth makes a difference when it comes to one's smile (the related photos are also from Dr. Huefner's website):

- The aging process can result in teeth wear and shortening coupled with a thinner upper-lip that tends to drop down, hiding some of the upper teeth. Lengthening the upper teeth with porcelain veneers can alleviate this issue and create a more youthful smile.

- When the patient's mouth is in a "repose" position with the teeth apart and jaws and lips relaxed, a younger adult will show 1-3 mm of teeth; therefore, lengthening the teeth for someone who is not showing teeth in a repose position can help to create a more vibrant smile.

- When the patient's mouth is in a full smile, the dentist can assess whether the upper teeth follow the curve of the smile line (bottom lip). If not, lengthening the teeth with porcelain veneers can create a more attractive smile that follows this curve, as can be seen in the photo below from one of my patients.resulted in beautiful, well-balanced smile.

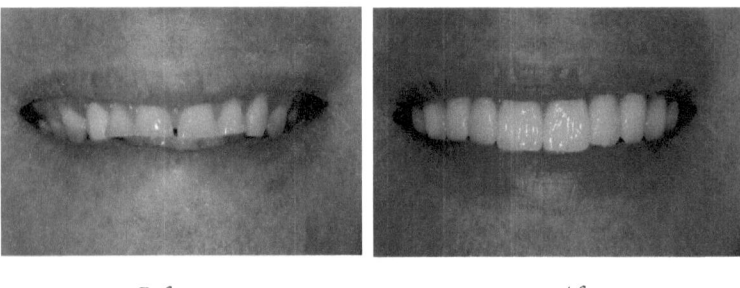

Before   *After*

The picture above is a great example of how the outline of the upper teeth should follow the lower lip to determine tooth length. The other way of determining adequate length is by observing how much tooth shows at a relaxed rest or repose. I created the diagrams below to help see what's normal.

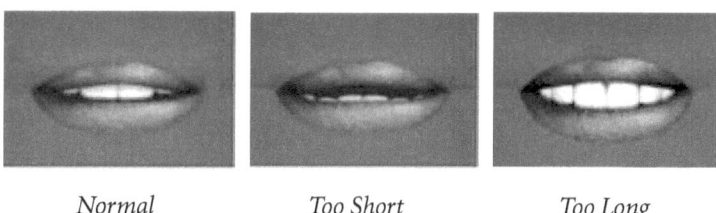

Normal   *Too Short*   *Too Long*

The right length of teeth depends on each person's individual facial shape and facial features. In other words, ideal tooth length will be unique to each person. Take a look at the photos below[73] to view the differences between teeth that are too short (top row), too long (bottom row) and properly proportioned (middle row):

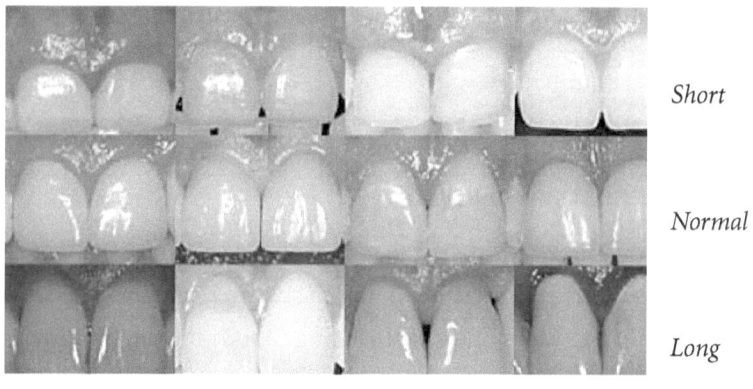

Short

Normal

Long

According to Dr. Huefner, the average teeth length is something cosmetic dentists should keep in mind. He explains:

The average length of an unworn upper central incisor is 10.5-11.5mm. A person with a smaller stature would more often use a smaller number, and likewise someone with a larger face a larger number. These averages are only used as a guide to reinforce to the patient that they are within some normal ranges. We've successfully made porcelain veneers for some patients as short as 9mm and as long as 15mm.

Determining the right length for each individual patient is a complicated process, but a qualified, experienced cosmetic dentist will be able to guide you through the process to create smile that is both beautiful and functional.

Components of the Smile Resources

"15 Fascinating Facts about Smiling": <http://www.pickthebrain.com/blog/15-fascinating-facts-about-smiling/>[74]

"Get the Best Smile for Your Face": http://www.sheknows.com/health-and-wellness/articles/814593/get-the-best-smile-for-your-face-1[75]

"Anatomy of a Smile": http://www.yourdentistryguide.com/smile-anatomy[76]

What is the Lips' Role in the Smile?

Our teeth communicate a message to those around us, but they aren't the only aspects of the smile doing the communicating. The lips also send certain messages and suggest things about the personality.

The lips are, in fact, highly expressive and greatly influence beauty as perceived by others. They contribute to the overall look of the face and influence the prominence and appearance of other facial features. As for personality, the lip size, shape and position send powerful non-verbal messages.

Author Rufenacht's (1990) book entitled *Fundamentals of Esthetics* in the section "Dental Components" shares the following information about the lips as they relate to personality:

- Thin upper and lower lips reflect self-control and satisfaction.

- Dominance of the lower lip reflects controlled and sensual ingeniousness.

- Equilibrium of upper and lower lips expresses characteristics of harmony, will and kindness.

- Thick upper and lower lips suggest an extroverted and easygoing personality.[77]

While there is not necessarily an ideal lip size or shape, there is an ideal lip line, which references how much of the teeth are exposed or covered by the lips. The ideal lip line is when the upper lip (in reference to the maxillary incisors) reaches the interdental gingival margin when smiling.[78] In other words, it is ideal to have the lips look like the "Normal Lip Line" in the following diagram.

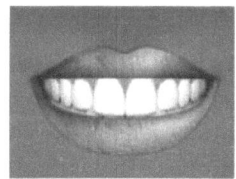 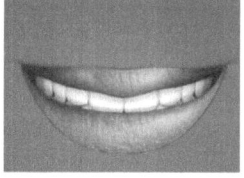 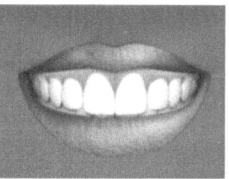

Normal Lip Line   *Low Lip Line*   *High Lip Line*

How Do Gums Impact the Smile?

In *Change Your Smile*, Goldstein (2009) discusses "gingival esthetics" and how the appearance and health of the gums impact the overall attractiveness of the smile[79]. Likewise, Rufenacht (1990) explains in *Fundamentals of Esthetics* that "healthy gingival tissue, as part of the biologic structural beauty, is an important factor of esthetic perception[80]".

If the gums appear unhealthy, discolored or are overexposed by the lips, it can take-away from the overall attractiveness of the face. Of course, there is also related health risk with gum disease, and research has linked it with increased cardiovascular disease and other illnesses.

Gum tissue should appear healthy, which means no red, puffy or bleeding gums. The preferred smile should not show more than three millimeters of gums between the top of your tooth and the bottom of your upper lip. The shape of the gums of the lower incisors and the upper laterals should be a symmetrical half-oval or half-circular shape. The upper centrals and canines should show a more oval, or elliptical, shape to the gums.

When it comes to the health and appearance of your gums, it is important to give them proper attention because they are very significant components of smile design. Issues such as excessive gingival exposure, uneven gum contours, inflammation and exposure of root surfaces are common gingival esthetic complaints that detract from your smile's attractiveness.

Additional Components of the Smile

Symmetry

Defined as the correspondence of opposite parts in size, shape and position (Guralink, 1982), there is horizontal symmetry and bilateral symmetry. Horizontal symmetry is when the teeth show similar elements from left to right in a regular sequence and have the same shape. In bilateral symmetry, the teeth design extends from a central point and the left and right are mirror images of each other.

Cosmetic dentists can work with an individual to achieve the ideal symmetry for one's facial structure and features.

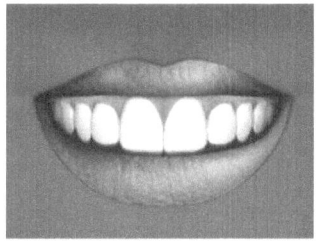 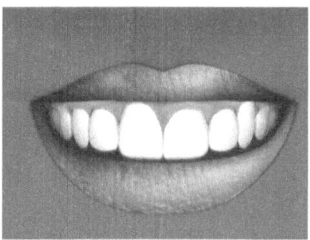

Normal   *Asymmetry*

Dental Midline

According to Lombardi (1973)[81], "the midline is an important focal point and, its proper placement is necessary for visual stability in an esthetic smile." The starting point of any cosmetic dental design is the facial midline, which is an imaginary vertical line drawn between the front two upper teeth. To achieve the optimal appearance, the facial midline should be in the middle of the face.

Whenever possible, the midline between the upper front teeth (central incisors) should coincide with the facial midline. In cases where this is not possible, the midline between the central incisors should be perpendicular to the imaginary line that could be drawn through the corners of the mouth[82].

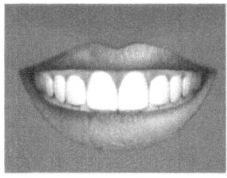  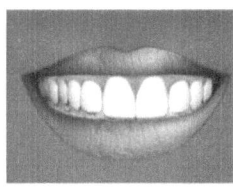 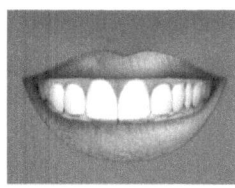

Normal Midline   *Midline to Right*   *Midline to Left*

Tooth Color

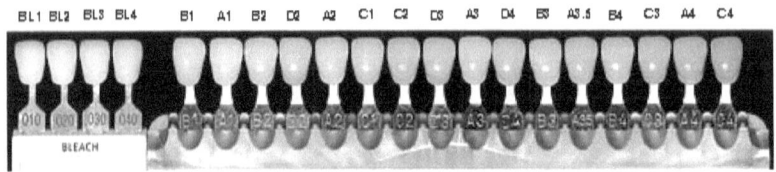

Tooth color also plays an important role in dental esthetics. In a study by Dunn et al. (1996), tooth color was considered to be the most important factor in predicting attractiveness. "Hue," "chroma," and "value" are the three dimensions of dental color.

It's clear by the enormous demand for teeth whitening products and services that tooth color has a great impact on an esthetically pleasing smile. Tooth color's impact on an esthetic smile is evident by the large demand in dentistry for whitening products.

According to the article "Anatomy of a Smile,"[83] the upper central incisors are the lightest and brightest teeth in your smile, whereas the upper side teeth are similar in color (hue) to that of the central incisors, but generally slightly lower in brightness (value). The canines (third teeth from midline) have greater intensity or saturation of color (chroma). First and second premolars (teeth behind canines), which are lighter and brighter than the canines, are similar in color to that of the lateral incisors.

As a dentist evaluates the color of your teeth, he or she will take a look at how closely-matched your upper and lower teeth are. The goal is to achieve a color/shade as close to natural esthetics as possible.

Embrasures

Embrasures are the little spaces in between the teeth where the teeth meet or join, and it forms a little inverted "V" on the upper teeth or a "V" on the lower teeth. These embrasures, in an ideal world, should progressively get larger from the front teeth to the back teeth. Having properly-sized embrasures help accentuate an attractive smile.

For example, if somebody has really worn teeth, they're going to have very little embrasures and oftentimes those embrasures will not progressively get larger, so that gives you a more masculine, mature-looking smile. In order to achieve a more youthful smile, it's very important to have properly spaced and sized embrasures.

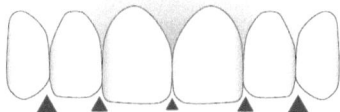

Normal progression of embrasures

Contact Height

Contact is the point at which the adjacent teeth meet. The position of the contact and the distance of that contact from the bone that supports the teeth dictates the level at which the gums will fill in between the teeth.

For example, if someone has a really high contact, chances are their gum tissues are not going to completely fill in that space between the two teeth. What may happen is they may end up having a space, or what we call a black triangle, which is basically a hole between the teeth where the gums don't fill in, and that typically is a very unattractive component of the smile.

People who are more prone to this teeth contact issue are people who have had previous gum problems, severe tooth wear or bad dental work. Other people at risk include those who have had quite a bit of tooth wear, meaning their teeth may have erupted, resulting in an increased contact height and lack of gum tissue filling the space.

It's important that the contact heights are correct in order to achieve adequate gum fill in between the teeth.

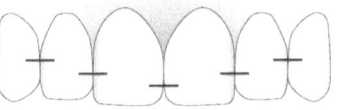

Normal Contact Heights

Teeth Angulation

Teeth should be symmetrical; they should not be rotated in any form or fashion. We don't want them to be too far out or too far in. From a profile viewpoint, we don't want the teeth to be sticking out too far in a bucktooth-fashion, and we also don't want them leaning in too far toward the tongue.

The way the tooth angulation should go in an ideal smile is that the back teeth, the molar teeth, should be angled in slightly toward the tongue and, as the smile goes forward, the angle should slowly tip back out to more of an upright angle in the front. The front teeth need to be angled more uprightly than the back teeth.

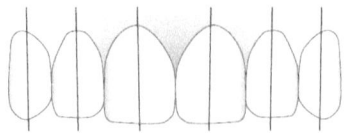

Normal Angulation

Central Dominance

What central dominance means is that ideally the front two teeth will be the stars of the stage, so to speak. They need to be slightly larger; they need to be slightly wider than the surrounding teeth. They need to be the dominant two things that you see when you smile.

There's a balance that you have to strike here because front teeth which are too dominant will give the appearance of somebody having rabbit teeth or buck teeth. It can very easily be a distracting feature in your smile. When I'm saying central dominance, I'm saying it is indeed a dominance, but it is a very *slight dominance* and so it's important that it be handled by professionals in just the right way in order to avoid overdoing it.

Smile Stories… Fixed at Last

My teeth used to be misaligned because I never visited a dentist when I was young. I can still remember my mother pulling out my teeth herself instead of bringing me to a dentist. She'd hoped to save money rather than paying for dental care. This eventually took a toll on my teeth because as my permanent teeth grew, they were misaligned.

When I was young, I didn't mind it but when I became a young adult, I became very self-conscious. My peers and classmates used to tease me about my teeth so I promised myself that one day, I would have them fixed.

That's exactly what I did when I got my first job – I went to a dentist and had my teeth fixed. It took some time, about four to six months. Now, whenever I see my friends, I am more confident. I am never shy about smiling at them because my teeth are now fixed.

I can still remember a boy who once teased me about my smile. Now he compliments my smile, thanks to my dentist!

Smile Stories… Ashamed No More

I have never had the best teeth in the world, and that's always made me feel less than confident. It is quite a traumatic life to lead when you are afraid to smile or laugh too fully for fear of your teeth showing.

When I was growing up my teeth were always slightly crooked and a little bit off-white which led me to be ashamed of them and embarrassed every time anyone would see them. I used to try to keep my mouth closed as much as possible and would often raise a hand to cover my mouth if I laughed out loud.

My teeth were very healthy, according to my dentist, but I hated them with a passion and would've listed them as the worst part of my body without a second thought. When I was a teenager my dentist suggested braces and whitening. As you would expect, I jumped at the change to improve my smile and lose my insecurity, and went ahead with the treatment.

The whitening came first and this alone made a massive difference to my life. Just having white teeth improved my confidence and made me less ashamed. The braces obviously took some time to work but in the end they did wonders for my teeth and made them almost as straight as a 'normal' person's. When they were taken off I felt like a different person. I wasn't ashamed or embarrassed at all and was actually proud of my mouth and how it looked. My life was transformed and those two simple procedures which enabled me to be a happy and confident person.

Smile Stories... Skateboarding Nightmare

A couple years ago I was skateboarding with some friends. I took a nasty fall when I was going fast down a hill, and I ended up falling off of my board and smashing face first into the concrete. My mouth took the brunt of the blow, and I knocked my two front teeth out.

The pain was incredibly difficult to deal with, but I was mostly concerned with how embarrassing it would be to open my mouth in the future and not have any front teeth. After my fall, I literally refused to smile, and most of the time I didn't even want to go out in public. I was ashamed of the way I looked.

Thankfully, my parents paid for the dental work to be done, and I went in a few weeks later for an appointment to have two replacement teeth put in. It was a fairly long process, but it was absolutely worth it. After having them put in, I no longer feel self-conscious about smiling in public, and I can act like myself again when I go out with my friends or on a date, and I don't have to worry about anyone ridiculing me because of the way my mouth looks.

Next

We've looked at the details of a smile, now we're going to explore the impact of smiling on kids and teens.

Chapter 8:

How Smiling Helps Kids and Teens

Golden slumbers kiss your eyes,
Smiles awake you when you rise.
Thomas Dekker, Author

A smile is one of the first gifts infants give their parents. It's a beautiful and natural way for them to show their love and happiness to others, and this doesn't end as they grow into toddlers, children and teens. However, along the way, various life experiences, insecurities and dental problems can inhibit their natural tendency to smile at the world around them.

By gaining an understanding of what the smile means to infants, children and teens and how it can impact their quality of life, it is easier to understand the importance of good dental hygiene, smile and dental care modeling, necessary dental procedures as well as how vital unconditional love and nurturing is from parents to their children.

Children and teens who feel confident in their smiles are better able to handle life's challenges, meet new people and provide a positive impression to those around them, which will benefit them throughout their lives.

When you see a child or teen who seems too embarrassed to smile or unable to smile, these are issues that need to be addressed. Of course, every child goes through phases, and one may be the "not smiling phase," but if this behavior goes on for months at a time, it could be a signal that you should give attention to the matter and seek out ways to bring the smile out in your child or teen—whether that be through dental procedures or increased parental involvement or even child or family counseling.

There are so many aspects to rearing healthy, self-confident children who choose to smile at life, and it is impossible, as parents, to get it right every step of the way. Yet, by reading this chapter and learning what you can do to give your child or teen the gift of a healthy smile, you are providing them with a very important tool they can use to make the most of their life experiences.

In the Beginning: Understanding an Infant's First Smile

According the article *Social Smile: An Interesting Comparison*[84] the social smile is the first milestone a child reaches, smiling within the first six weeks of birth. Other milestones tend to follow in quick succession after that first social smile. It's almost like a domino effect.

A delay in the social smile, especially if it is beyond three months of age, may be a sign indicating a neurological or developmental problem. The author explains:

> *Between six and ten weeks, a social smile emerges, usually accompanied by other pleasure-indicative actions and sounds, including cooing and mouthing. This social smile occurs in response to adult smiles and interactions. As infants become more aware of their environment, smiling occurs in response to a*

wider variety of contexts. Smiles are considered to serve a developmental function.

Smile attachment theories suggest that an infant's smile is a way to interact with caregivers. Authors Patricia C. Broderick and Pamela Blewitt explain in *The Life Span: Human Development for Helping Professionals* (2009) that babies give more smiles to their primary caregivers than to any other person. It is because they feel a deep connection to these caregivers and receive the smiles and attention in return.

When an infant smiles at the caregiver, and the caregiver returns the smile, the infant's emotional state is likely to remain positive, which in turn opens them up for further social engagement[85] with the caregiver as well as others in their life.

It's easy to see that those early years provide a great opportunity for parents to instill a healthy smile in their children. Parents who have a fearful or negative facial expression on a regular basis may inhibit their child's tendency to smile.

"Infants use the emotional information provided by caregivers to help them interpret situations that are ambiguous to them" (p. 113). Essentially, as a parent or primary caregiver, you have the unique opportunity to shape your child's ability to smile at life and to understand positive and negative behavior, not only when they are infants, but as they grow into children, teens and adults.

Infant Smiles: Video Resources

How an Infant Learns Behavior through Smiles and Facial Expressions of Others: http://www.youtube.com/watch?v=p6cqNhHrMJA&tracker=False

Baby Lila's First Smiles: http://www.youtube.com/watch?v=hp-V5xWVPfU

Baby Development Milestones: http://www.youtube.com/watch?v=HNizU5Jbhuw

Social Smiles: http://www.youtube.com/watch?v=HzmWAi_5Q9o

Still Face Experiment: http://www.youtube.com/watch?v=apzXGEbZht0

Attunement and Why It Matters: http://www.youtube.com/watch?v=URpuKgKt9kg&feature=related

---

Social Implications of a Smile for Kids and Teens

An infant's experience with smiling in the early developmental stages directly impacts his or her smile as a child and teen. It is typically the teen years when more problems and social issues develop in regards to the smile. An individual may go through the childhood years smoothly, only to hit the teen years and struggle with low self-confidence, social awkwardness, dental problems and other issues that contribute to a less than ideal smile.

A healthy smile is a teen's best asset. It does more than just reflect kindness to others, it providers the smiler with increased confidence and gives them an emotional boost, so they feel better about themselves and their outlook on life improves.

Because today's kids and teens are so tuned in to celebrities and their appearances, there is increased desire among youth to have nice smiles. When all they see around them are straight, white teeth—on Facebook, in magazines, on movies—they will feel self-conscious if they have teeth that do not look the same.

By teaching kids and teens good oral health, we can take a big step in helping them to feel more free and comfortable smiling, which will help them to feel better about life in general.

Most teens know many friends who have had braces and other dental work done to improve their smiles, so being able to access this type of care themselves is important. It seems that teenage girls are especially aware of this, although it can be the same for many boys.

In the study entitled "Influence of Dental Esthetics on Social Perceptions of Adolescents Judged By Peers"[86] Researchers Henson, Lindauer, Gardner, Shroff, Tufekci and Best found that photographs of individuals with ideal smile esthetics were consistently rated higher on average that images of individuals with non-ideal smiles.

The rating categories were broken down into perceptions of athletic performance, popularity and leadership ability. The researchers concluded that "on average, ratings for the ideal smiles in perceived athletic, social, and leadership skills were about 10% higher than those given for images with nonideal smiles."[87]

This study went on to explain how dental procedures, particularly orthodontic treatment, focused on creating more beautiful smiles would provide "modest social benefits for adolescent patients" (Am J Orthod Dentofacial Orthop 2011; 140:389-95).

This makes a great case for giving your kids the best chance at a good impression on peers through optimizing their smile.

Making Friends with a Smile

It is safe to say that everyone, especially children and teens, wants to be accepted. A simple, healthy smile can actually help kids to feel more accepted in two ways:

1. When putting a smile on his face, a teen will feel more attractive and intelligent—this act of self-contentment is evident in a smile, and makes the teen feel better about himself than he would without a smile.

2. When smiling, the teen is expressing joy, happiness and friendliness to others, which is most often reciprocated back to her. She smiles, someone smiles back at her, and she feels accepted.

As we've covered in previous chapters, a smile has the power to set off a cycle of friendliness, self-acceptance, acceptance of others, and sharing positive feelings with others. However, a person without a smile is unable to begin or participate in this cycle.

We look back to the story of the young man named Phillip we discussed in Chapter 2. He really struggled in social situations at school. Others seemed to exclude him and ignore him, even his teachers were less-than-friendly towards him. He didn't get it and wondered why everyone treated him that way. The fact was that Phillip had never learned to utilize his most powerful communication tool: his smile. He didn't smile, therefore, others did not interact with him, or when they did they were not pleasant towards him.[88]

The desire to be liked by others drives many youth to do things they would normally not do and can lead them to succumb to negative influences. Encouraging children and teens to discover and utilize their smiles is a way to avoid low-self-esteem that can lead to negative peer pressure.

An article entitled *10 Confidence Boosters for Teens*[89] listed "smile" as the number two tip for increasing self-esteem, explaining: "Even if it is the last thing you feel like doing, keep smiling. Try and look for little things to smile about, smile at strangers. Just the act of smiling releases endorphins into your bloodstream." These endorphins can elevate mood, providing the teen with a better outlook on life.

However, teaching youth to smile must go beyond encouraging a "fake smile" that they should use even when they are feeling negative emotions. Experts on facial expressions are not fooled by the big, fake smile. A true smile—the natural Duchenne smile—is the involuntary smile that engages the muscles around the eyes.

As parents and caregivers, adults can give their children unconditional love and acceptance, while encouraging them to discover and use their smiles. Giving them the experience of love, humor and friendship is a way to facilitate the Duchenne smile that will serve them well in their lives and as they build relationships with others.

Helping Teens to Achieve Healthy Self-Esteem, Healthy Smile

Every person goes through many changes, transitions and struggles in life, but studies show that teens are often more significantly affected by these life experiences than adults. They tend to feel emotions more deeply and allow situations to shape their worldviews and self-perceptions.

The teen years are an extremely influential time in the life of an individual, and how a teen responds to these years can impact the way he views himself for the rest of his life. Academic scores or performance-based activities play a role in a teen's self-esteem, but some teens who excel in these areas still struggle to have a healthy self-perception.

Appearance is another biggie. Teens are judged by their peers based on physical appearance. Of course, we wish the world was not this way, but it's the way that it is, and parents can help their teens to optimize their appearances in order to improve their self-esteem and give them the best chance possible for relational success.

Still, we must teach them that body image is not the key to everything, and a perfect appearance is not essential to success. During the teenage years, a teen is learning to become comfortable in her skin. As we live in a society that puts beauty and the "fat-free look" on a pedestal and teens are greatly impacted by this. Even teens who are physically fit and beautiful by society's standards, feel inferior, because they compare themselves to air-brushed images in magazines and in the media.

We can show teens that the different appearances, shapes, types of beauty are what make the world interesting. Teach them that we do not need to look like air-brushed models to be beautiful and that true beauty comes from within.

What can parents, caregivers and teachers do to counteract this? We can show teens that the different appearances, shapes, types of beauty are what make the world interesting. Teach them that we do not need to look like air-brushed models to be beautiful and that true beauty comes from within. It can be difficult for teens to accept and absorb this message, so it is important to keep it coming and facilitate conversations about the topic often.

Experts advise parents and caregivers to help teens improve their self-esteem in a gradual manner—avoiding extreme highs and lows, which can lead to depression. Instead of focusing on one aspect of the child's appearance, performance, etc., focus on teaching the teen how she can feel good about herself as a whole human being.

It is important to teach teens healthy self-esteem by example. Often, negative self-esteem issues are a result of teens having parents who tend to have poor self-esteem themselves. Just like infants who mimic their parents' smiles, teens will mimic the parents' self-perceptions.

For example, if a parent is continually complaining about his own appearance, a child will pick that up and speak the same way about himself when he looks in the mirror. If a parent speaks about herself using self-disparaging comments, it is likely the teen with follow suit. When we, as adults, can learn to treat ourselves with love and respect, improving our own self-esteem, the youth we influence will emulate this behavior.

Teens need to know that they do not have to be perfect to be accepted and loved. We can teach them to celebrate their strong points and successes while being forgiving of shortcomings they may have—this includes all areas of their lives, not just academics or competitive sports.

Place value on teens for who they are as human beings, not just on what they do. Point out positive characteristics and personality traits, such as:

- "You have a great sense of humor!"
- "I really enjoy hearing you talk about the books you read."
- "You showed your caring personality tonight when you helped your brother."

What does all this talk about self-esteem have to do with the all-powerful communication tool, the smile? If teens have a foundation of positive self-esteem, the smile will come naturally…

www.SmilingSuccess.com/2freegifts

By focusing on positive personal characteristics, rather than on performance-based activities, you are reinforcing the idea that the teen is a valuable person, worthy of appreciation and love, because of who they are—not on their level of success or physical appearance.

On the flip side, it is okay to share constructive criticism with teens, but it must be balanced out with confidence-boosting talk. Don't expect your criticism to be effective if there is no love or praise behind it. However, teens must learn that criticism is part of life, so it is beneficial for you to teach them how to handle it and use it without taking it personally or letting it crush them.

What does all this talk about self-esteem have to do with the all-powerful communication tool, the smile? If teens have a foundation of positive self-esteem, the smile will come naturally.

When they feel good about themselves and who they are as human beings, they won't have to fake smiles. Rather, the natural Duchenne smile will emerge, and this natural smile will help them to better relate to others, have more opportunities to experience new things, and get the most out of the teen years.

Smile[90]

Awhile.
Why not?
Forgot?
Give yourself a moment's rest.
Smiling helps us be our best.
Not allowing outside things,
To get us down, or clip our wings.
For we are children of the One,
So don't deprive yourself true fun
For in its spirit we can be
Victors for eternity.

www.SmilingSuccess.com/2freegifts

Smile[91]

For some it's hard.
For others it's easy.
We can allow it to be subtle.
Most of the time it's cheesy.

Use it to say a flirty hello;
Or a lingering goodbye.
Try to make a newborn stop crying;
Or say hi to a loved one in the sky.

No matter how you do it;
For a second or a while.
Just look at the camera...
Smile.

How to Help Teens Achieve Their Ideal Healthy Smile

While a smile is important in so many ways to a teen's quality of life and outlook on life, if they feel ashamed of their teeth it may be difficult for them to put their smile to good use. As parents and caregivers, we can encourage them to take the necessary steps to have a healthy smile that begins with the foundation of good dental hygiene and care.

The bright smiles they likely see on celebrities and other faces they admire are achievable for them if they can get into a consistent routine, involving the following:

- Flossing regularly.

- Regular dentist visits to deal with cavities and other dental issues that can impact their best smiles possible.

- Teeth straightening procedures.

- Whitening treatments—professional in-office treatment is safest and most effective.

> View one mom's testimonial to see how the right dental care and procedures can improve a child's smile and outlook on life: http://beautyandbedlam.com/importance-of-a-smile[92]

It is important as parents and caregivers to model good oral hygiene to children and teens. When they see dental care is part of your daily routine, it will influence them to do the same, and is much more impactful than strongly worded messages.

When it comes to more in-depth dental care, orthodontic treatment may be necessary to help children and teens achieve their ideal smile the can give with confidence. A study entitled "Psychological Influences on the Timing of Orthodontic Treatment"[93] discusses the personality characteristics, motives and aesthetic values of young patients in regards to orthodontic care. It specifically analyzes children's perceived reasons for treatment and revealed that both children and their parents expected the most improvement in self-image, oral function and social life.

Children rated faces with crowded teeth, overbite and diastema negatively. The results of the study revealed that younger children are indeed good candidates for orthodontics and expect the procedures to improve their lives.

Even the high expectations for orthodontic treatment shows that children and parents believe the children can have a better life experience when their teeth are healthy and as beautiful as they can be.

A study from Qualtrough and Burk (1994), found that more than 70% of the parents surveyed considered orthodontic treatment important to their child's ultimate success in future careers and believed that the child would be more attractive and better liked as a result of the treatment.[94]

70% of the parents surveyed considered orthodontic treatment important to their child's ultimate success in future careers and believed that the child would be more attractive and better liked as a result of the treatment.

Another study entitled "Does Orthodontic Treatment Affect Patients' Quality of Life?"[95] follows up on these expectations, reporting that orthodontists should consider these expectations as they move forward with treatments: "Regardless of age, patients' and their parents' or caregivers' expectations about improvements in oral function, esthetics, social acceptance, and body image are important for both general dentists and orthodontists to consider when advising patients about these procedures and during the treatment process."

Working with a dentist or orthodontist who can help to meet your expectations is an important step in achieving the results you and your child desire. It is perfectly fine to interview candidates to determine which professional is right for you. The best choice will be in tune with your expectations and have a full understanding of what these procedures mean to you and your child or teen.

Common Teen Dental Issues

From bad breath and braces to teeth whitening and straightening, there a number of procedures available to teens to help them achieve their best smile.

Let's take a look at some of the common dental issues and procedures teens face:

- Braces are important for achieving straight teeth, which provides for a more balanced facial appearance, but straight teeth are also easier to clean, which promotes healthier gums. Straightened teeth are also less likely to get chipped than crooked or slanted teeth.

- Today's teens see nice, white teeth all around them, not only in the media, but also on friends. Teeth bleaching is becoming very popular, but it is not a safe procedure to try at home, because the products can cause gum irritation or tooth sensitivity. Some of the over-the-counter whitening products aren't even effective, so it is best to seek professional care.

- Teens can be very sensitive about bad breath issues, also known as halitosis, and for good reason. In order to have the confidence to be around friends, they want to have fresh breath. Regular dentist visits and good oral hygiene habits can help teens to achieve a healthy mouth that leads to fresh breath.[96]

How a Healthy Smile Creates a Good First Impression for Teens

As we've covered in previous chapters, the smile is one of the most powerful tools in creating a good first impression for adults, but this is also true for teens. First impressions when it comes to teachers and friends are responsible for setting the tone for the interactions and relationships the child or teen will have with them during her life.

Interestingly, this is true even for infants, which goes to show exactly how influential first impressions can be throughout one's life. According to Corter et al. (1973) revealed physical attractiveness impacts individuals immediately after birth, as nurses give higher intellectual prognoses to infants they perceive to be more physically attractive.[97]

The thesis explains: "There is also evidence that attractive children are preferred over unattractive children by their teachers (Clifford and Walster, 1973)…"[98]

Healthy teeth with the right dental and orthodontic care when necessary prepare children and teens to make the best first impressions possible, which will set them up for success in various life experiences and relationships.

How to Make a Great First Impression[99]

Can you make somebody like you in less than a minute? Or even less? Apart from the amount of time that is needed to make a great first impression, you should realize the following fact.

First impression gives description about your aggressiveness, attractiveness, character, competence, likeability, personality and trustworthiness toward others…Based on several studies, most of us judge on someone's character and personality based on their first impression. Like it or not, judgments according to first appearance make a powerful role in how people treat others, and how we get treated.

Here are several suggestions which might help you to make a great first impression.

1. **Smile**—Smiling is the easiest way to create a great first impression. Smile means a good self-confidence, happiness,

---

enthusiasm and acceptance. When we smile, we express our self-confidence toward others. Happiness is felt by everyone around us while we smile. Give a genuine smile and you will spread enthusiasm. Enthusiasm is contagious and brings out the best in you to the others. Finally, by giving a genuine smile, everyone feels that you will accept their appearance at most of the time.

2. **Laugh**—Laughter is the best medicine for your heart and infectious too. When you laugh, you will bind people together, increase happiness and intimacy.

3. **Time**—Time does matter when you want to create a great first impression. Moreover, you only have 100 milliseconds to create your good impressions (Todorov and Willis, 2006). Prepare your first ten seconds to your best ability. Smile plus a good body posture would be a good combination to reach the goal.

4. **Words**—Pick your first words carefully. Use words which describe positivity so that people would have a great impression about you.

> **Source:** Teen Advice (n.d.). How to make a great first impression. *Ygoy.* Retrieved April 3, 2012, from http://teenadvice.ygoy.com/2010/05/18/how-to-make-a-great-first-impression/

A Healthy Smile: The Foundation for a Healthy, Fulfilled Life

At first glance, the statement that a smile could be a foundation for a fulfilled life may seem like a stretch, but when you examine the different aspects of the smile and the power it holds in the life of a child or a teen, it is easy to see that a smile truly holds the key to richer relationships and life experiences.

Because children and teens have busy, active lives and often do not give a second thought to the health of their teeth, it is the caregiver's responsibility to teach them about good oral hygiene as well as model it to them. Furthermore, guiding children and teens to achieve healthy self-esteems and positive self-images will enable them to optimize the use of their smiles to make the most of it now and throughout their lives.'

Smile Stories… A Restored Smile and Renewed Hope[100]

Meet Zeb, a promising Brooklyn high school student who once suffered pain and embarrassment from the effects of poor oral health. He dreaded getting his photo taken and meeting new people, fearing ridicule once they saw his unsightly smile. Facing an uncertain future and feeling his dreams of a better life slipping away, he said, "I wish I could smile without feeling ashamed." His damaged self-esteem and shaken confidence were holding him back. He wondered how he could become successful in life if he was too ashamed to smile confidently in an interview situation.

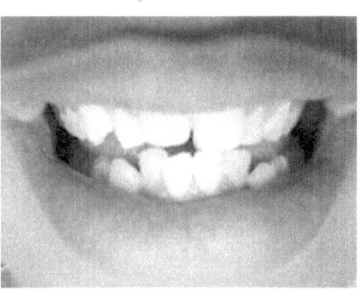

Zeb Before

Lacking the resources to get the dental treatment he desperately needed, Zeb and his mother turned to *Tomorrow's SMILES*®, a teen program of the National Children's Oral Health Foundation: *America's Toothfairy*® (NCOHF), for help.

Through this NCOHF program, Zeb was introduced to Dr. Anthony Ramirez and his team. Little did he realize just how much this *Tomorrow's SMILES* volunteer dentist and his team would change his life. His journey to a happy, healthy future was about to begin.

Poor oral health can be devastating for an adolescent struggling to fit in and prepare for a successful future. Zeb is not alone in this struggle. In fact, 23% of adolescents aged 12 to 19 years have untreated decay. Distracted by pain and embarrassment, simple things like concentrating in school or making friends become tremendous challenges for these teens, hindering their academic and social development. Even more disturbing are the effects this can have on their future. Their struggles of today can shatter their hopes and dreams for their future.

Zeb After

Tomorrow's SMILES was designed to give teens like Zeb the building blocks they need for healthy, productive futures by providing them with life-changing oral health services. Through this innovative program sponsored by the Patterson Foundation, volunteer dentists provide pro bono services to promising at-risk teens in their community, restoring their self-esteem and encouraging them to take responsibility for their oral health. *Tomorrow's SMILES* volunteer dentists also have access to generously donated products from Invisalign® and Nobel Biocare™ (including Procera®) to help restore the smiles of pre-screened, promising teens.

Zeb is now attending his first year of college on a full scholarship. "I have been blessed with an incredible gift," remarked Zeb about his restored, beautiful smile and renewed hope for a future filled with possibilities ahead.

You can help transform a teen's needless pain and suffering into a happy, beautiful smile and the promise of a brighter future by encouraging your practice to volunteer services for *Tomorrow's SMILES*. Visit www.TomorrowsSMILES.org or email Brenda Woodington at bwoodington@ncohf.org to learn more about this life-changing program!

Next

Let's move from kids and teens to practical steps on how to improve your smile.

Chapter 9:

How to Improve Your Smile

A smile is a curve that sets everything straight.
Phyllis Diller, American Actress & Comedian

Whether you started reading this book in hopes of helping yourself, a child, a teen or another loved one to reap the benefits of a beautiful, healthy smile, there is one thing left to get you on track to meet your goal: an action plan. While information and knowledge is important, taking action is the key to experiencing the desired results.

Your specific action plan will depend upon the unique needs you possess, and in this chapter, we will help you to assess those needs and guide you in creating an effective plan. You may have ideas in mind for how you can improve your smile, but it can help you define exactly what you want by conducting a self-analysis and an objective dental survey. You'll also want to be sure you understand the details of the dental procedures and options available to you.

In previous chapters, we have addressed the major players or components of the smile:

- Lips
- Teeth

- Gums

- Eyes and muscles surrounding the eyes.

Each of these components plays an important role in the smile and greatly impacts the level of attractiveness of the smile as well as the message communicated by the smile. For this reason, as we consider the dental procedures and options available, we will pay attention to these individual components and the smile as a whole.

Smile Self-Analysis

Using the 21 principles of smile design, this self-analysis will help you to know how to identify problematic aspects of your smile, enabling you to determine what dental procedures you may utilize to maximize your smile.

Created by MyHealthReport Patient Report and Education Center[101], the assessment goes through all of the smile design parameters one-by-one. To complete the exercise, you will need a mirror, a millimeter ruler, and if possible a close-up – photo of your smile. Review each principle and take note of the principles containing criteria your smile does not meet.

Top of Form

⌐   Width: Height Ratio

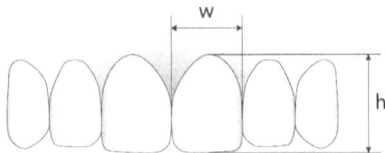

The width:height ratio for the front incisor teeth should be 75-80 %. This means the front of the incisor teeth should be taller than they are wider, like a rectangle sitting upright or on its end. For example, if the width were 8.0 mm and the height 10 mm, the ratio (8/10) would equal 80%.

Mesial Inclination

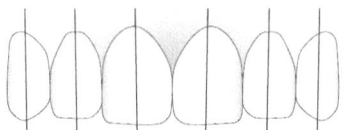

Each upper tooth visible in the smile should have a slight inclination or toed-in tilt that is toward the midline of the mouth. If each of these imaginary lines on the front teeth were extended downward, they would meet or converge at or near the navel point over the abdomen.

Midline Placement

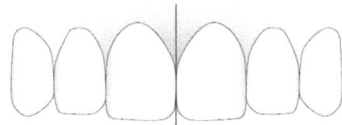

The positioning of the midline between the two front central incisor teeth should be on a line drawn from between the eyes and down through the nose, lips, and chin. Furthermore, the cant or angle of this midline should not be tilted to the left or right, but should be straight up and down.

Color, Shadings, Stains & Markings

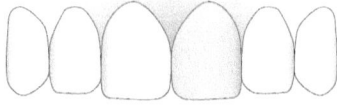

All visible teeth should be of a uniform color or shade, preferably on the lighter side. Smiles are compromised when one or more teeth are darker than the rest, or when there are white or dark spots or markings on the enamel.

Smile at Rest

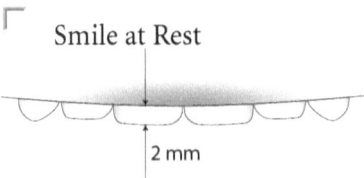

2 mm

Middle-aged adults should show 2-4 mm of the bottom of their upper teeth when at rest or when slightly smiling. This amount slightly decreases with age as the "window" of the mouth begins to sag downward, showing more of the lower teeth in the smile window.

Gum Line Symmetry

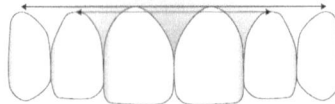

The gum tissue frames the teeth and forms a "curtain" for the teeth. The height and scalloping of the gum line should be symmetrical or matched evenly between the left and right sides. Balance and symmetry are important parts of what makes an attractive smile.

Gum Line Margin Heights

The height or position of the gum line over the upper lateral incisors should be slightly lower than the height of the gums positioned over the adjacent central incisor and canine tooth.

Gaps or Diastema

A diastema is a gap or spacing between the teeth. It can happen because of teeth which are too small for the amount of space available in the upper or lower jaw, and/or because of misaligned or crooked teeth.

Gummy Smile

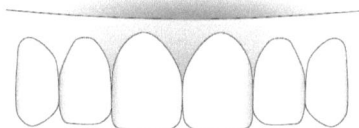

A "gummy smile" is when too much gum tissue shows above your front teeth when you smile. Ideally there should be only a slight amount of gum tissue showing above the front teeth when you smile.

Gingival Zenith

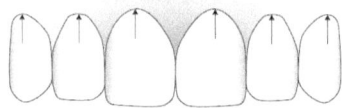

The height or position of the gum line as it tracks across the face of each tooth varies from tooth to tooth. The "zenith" or highest point should be in the center of each lateral incisor, and should be 2/3rds of the way (toward the next tooth back) across the face of the central incisors and canine teeth.

Smile Line Follows Lower Lip

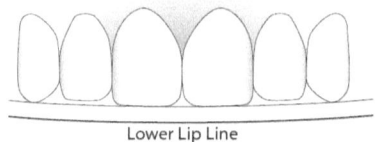

Lower Lip Line

The smile line (the incisal or biting edge) of the upper front teeth should parallel or generally follow the contour of a normal lower lip in a relaxed or slight smile.

Horizontal Plane

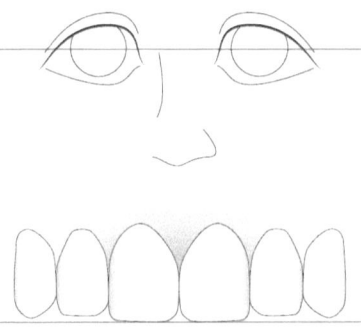

The left to right horizontal biting plane of the mouth should parallel the floor or horizon when standing. It likewise should parallel a line drawn between the eyes (the inter-pupillary line). The horizontal plane from the front to the back of the mouth should also generally parallel the floor. (Note: Some people's eyes and ears are not naturally on a level plane.)

Gum Tissue Health/Bad Breath

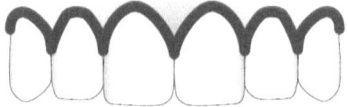

www.SmilingSuccess.com/2freegifts

Healthy gums do not bleed and are light pink in color and are stippled in texture (like an orange peel). Gum disease is linked to heart disease. It can also be very unsightly, smelly and socially offensive! Oral bacteria cause tooth decay, gum disease and bad breath! Any plan for an attractive smile and good oral health must include necessary gum therapy and/or regular dental maintenance along with good oral hygiene practices to promote and maintain good gum health.

Contact Points

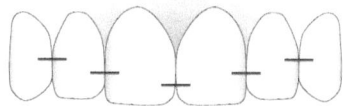

Each tooth should touch its neighbor tooth at a contact point which 'snaps' when flossed. This contact point should be positioned near the biting edge of the two upper central incisors, and gradually move upward in its position with each tooth contact, moving toward the canine teeth.

Malalignment or Crowding

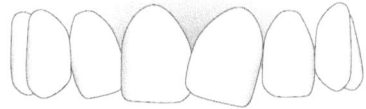

Teeth should be straight and fit evenly side by side. Crooked and crowded teeth are harder to maintain and create an unkempt appearance in the smile. Crowding happens when there isn't enough room for teeth or when the jaws are too small, often due to growth and development problems. Bone loss and tooth loss can also cause teeth to be uneven.

Incisal Embrasure

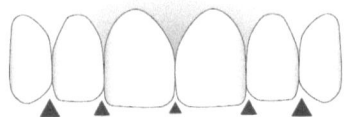

The corners of each tooth create a point of separation from its neighboring tooth. This outline shape between the front teeth forms a triangle silhouette appearance. This is best seen as a triangle shape wedge between the teeth and on the biting edge of the front teeth. Each incisal embrasure or triangle should be symmetrical with its opposite left/right side counterpart, and should increase in size moving back away from the midline.

Golden Proportion

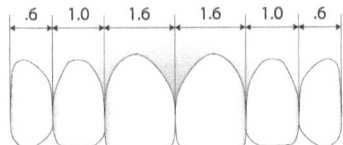

As in nature, the proportion principle follows the "rule of thirds". Each tooth away from the midline should be two-thirds as wide as the previous tooth when viewed straight on from the front. Proportion plays an essential role in creating a balanced and pleasing look to the eye. When teeth and smiles are properly proportioned it creates a dimension of beauty seen and mimicked in nature known as the "golden proportion".

Black Triangle

A dark see-through "black triangle" appears between the front teeth at the gum line when the teeth are too far apart or the underlying bone level dissolves away. When this happens, the gum papilla shrinks and allows the darkness from the back of the mouth to show through as a dark triangle.

⌐ Vertical Dimension

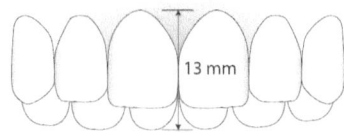

The loss of vertical dimension can make you look older. The vertical distance between the nose and the chin can be shortened due to improper growth, the teeth have been worn down or become missing. When the jaws and dental bite are properly positioned it creates a vertical proportion to the lower part of the face that is pleasing to the eye and generally healthy for the jaws and jaw joints.

⌐ Dark Silver Mercury Fillings

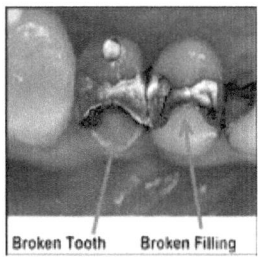

Silver-mercury fillings tend to expand and contract over time. This can cause cracks to form which can weaken and damage the tooth. Dark metal fillings also cast a dark shadow through the tooth and blemish the smile.

Old Dentistry

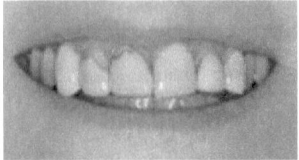

Older dental fillings and crown restorations can experience wear and break down just as do the teeth they have restored. Dark lines at the edges of old porcelain crowns become more visible when gums recede. Old porcelain crowns often lack a natural vital appearance and appear more opaque and white when compared with natural teeth next to them. Old composite fillings can yellow or darken as they age. Modern cosmetic materials and methods can restore and update an aged or worn-out smile and create a natural looking smile.

You can either use the results from your self-assessment as a discussion piece at your next dentist appointment, or go to the website at http://333.myhealthreport.info/rac/cosmetic-smile-self-analysis-calculator.php to receive a full report about your assessment. Either way, taking the time to conduct the self-assessment is a great first step to identifying potential problems with your smile. This will help you know where to begin as you work with your dentist to create your best smile possible.

Dental Options to Improve Your Smile

Many options exist for improving the dental quality of the teeth and smile, such as orthodontic treatments, replacements and even surgical procedures. In order to determine which dental option is right for your unique situation, it is important to have an understanding of what is available to you.

Below is a list of options for you to consider and discuss with your dental care provider, so you can begin to map out your action plan for your best smile possible.

Invisalign/Traditional Braces

Orthodontic treatments such as Invisalign or traditional braces are very powerful ways to reorient crooked teeth, straighten up teeth, improve teeth function and to enhance the smile overall.

While most are familiar with traditional braces, Invisalign is a lesser known dental option. It is a series of clear aligners that snap-fit over teeth. The wearer changes up the liners every two weeks and with each aligner there is programmed movement of the individual teeth, moving the teeth slightly over time, resulting in the desired teeth position and characteristics.

The company, Align, sends a computer-animated model to each patient receiving the treatment, illustrating the movement of teeth from start to finish. This enables the patient to see the end-result of the treatment before he or she even begins. The smooth edges of the aligners mean that the patient will not have to deal with the sore inner mouth and lips typical of traditional braces.

Invisalign is very powerful and effective and is actually one of the most conservative ways to improve the smile without doing any kind of significant alteration of the tooth structure. A major draw for many adult patients is the fact that it is virtually invisible. Whether you are a business man, socialite, salesperson or a company CEO, you can straighten your teeth without unsightly metal braces.

Traditional braces can still get the job done with the metal brackets and wires, but they can be uncomfortable, even painful, and a hassle with food getting stuck in them. With the Invisalign option available, most adults and teens are finding that it is an option that fits in better with their lifestyles.

Of course, for some kids and teens, traditional braces may be a preferred option, particularly if compliance is an issue. You cannot remove traditional braces, but you can remove the Invisalign aligners, so parents will need to consider this factor when making the choice.

While it has been a concern in the past that Invisalign was somewhat limited in what it could do treatment-wise, their new technology can correct nearly any case as well as traditional braces. Even surgical cases can be treated with Invisalign.

Veneers

Veneers are thin porcelain pieces that fit over existing teeth. The teeth often have to be prepared ever so slightly for veneers. In some cases, there can be veneers placed on your teeth that require no preparation of your teeth, but typically some preparation is necessary.

The beauty of veneers is how extremely flexible they are in terms of what we can accomplish with them. I like to call veneers the workhorses of the cosmetic industry, because with veneers, we can alter the rotation, length, width, color, and contour of the teeth. They're such powerful tools in improving a smile.

Ideal candidates for veneers are people who have chipping and severe discolorations that cannot be improved with whitening or tetracycline staining. Other great patients for this procedure are people who simply do not want to go through six months to a year-and-a-half of Invisalign or traditional braces. They often opt for veneers because veneers can be completed in as little as two or three weeks.

The preparation of the teeth for veneers involves removing a little bit of the existing tooth structure to make room for the veneer, thus, preventing overly bulky or large teeth post-veneers. We have to prepare the tooth in a very specific shape to get it ready for the process.

The preparations are usually very thin. It can be as thin as a 0.5 mm or less in some situations. In other situations where there is a lot of rotation of the teeth or if the teeth are inclined in a certain way we may have to prepare the tooth more in order to give the appearance that that tooth is straight even though it is actually rotated or crooked.

Benefits to veneers include:

- Extremely durable and long-lasting with a life expectancy of anywhere from 10 to 12 years
- Stain-resistant
- Treat veneers just like you treat natural teeth

Whitening

Whitening is probably the most popular and the most common way of kicking your smile up a notch. Whitening is simple, safe, and can be extremely effective. It's clear to see from the amount of money put into advertising for teeth whitening products that it is a very powerful tool.

There are numerous over-the-counter methods, but most of the whitening toothpastes out there do not have a big impact on changing the color of your teeth. Any shade change or whitening is very minor. No matter what the brand name of the product, these over-the-counter products are not nearly as effective as a professional in-office whitening product that comes with a customized tray, prescription-strength whitening gel and close monitoring by the dentist.

Another great method is Zoom whitening or laser whitening. These two methods incorporate a special light source, either laser or a specifically keyed light to a certain wavelength, in order to activate the whitening gel to achieve a better penetration or a deeper whitening effect of your teeth.

Zoom or laser whitening usually requires about an hour or so of your time in a dental office and can be extremely effective, particularly for people who want to get their whitening done immediately. Over-the-counter products can take a long time to whiten teeth.

With in-office professional whitening, you walk in with yellow teeth and walk out with nice pearly whites. The beautiful thing about in-office whitening is that most dentists will give you the trays to continue touching up or to continue whitening at home until you achieve your desired effect.

Tooth Replacement

A lot of people simply have missing teeth, which is where tooth replacement comes in as an important dental procedure.

An interesting story regarding the power of tooth replacement: I was watching the show "X Factor." There was a contestant who was a cute gal and a great singer. She had a tooth missing on the left side of her mouth, so every time she would smile big or she would sing there was a very unattractive gap in her smile. And those types of gaps can be corrected in a lot of cases with dental implants.

Three reasons why dental implants are so effective:

1. They restore beauty

2. They restore function

3. They also help prevent bone loss in the jaw bone due to the jaw bone not being stimulated from having a tooth present.

For people who have sunken-in lips, are lacking lip support because they're missing teeth, have collapsing teeth or are experiencing problematic speech issues as a result of missing teeth, dental implants are the way to go.

If a dental implant is not possible, then a dental bridge is another option. A bridge is like having two dental crowns with one crown in between connected together. The bridge fits over the two existing teeth on either side of the missing teeth and is cemented permanently in place. The drawback is that dental bridges are typically not as long-lasting as an implant.

Crowns

While crowns have been a dental option for years, now with all of the available technology in terms of our porcelain systems and how accurately we can mimic nature, crowns have resurfaced as one of the most popular ways of correcting cosmetic issues, second only to veneers. The difference between a crown and a veneer is that a crown wraps all the way around the tooth, whereas a veneer just covers the front part of the tooth and sometimes the sides of the teeth.

Why someone would choose a crown versus a veneer depends upon several factors:

- What kind of condition is the tooth in?
- Does the tooth have large existing restorations?
- Does it already have an old-style unaesthetic crown?
- Is the tooth severely rotated or severely leaning to one way or another?

If one or more of the above scenarios exists, it is likely necessary to do a crown on the tooth in order to achieve an attractive result. Crowns can be utilized in conjunction with veneers. In some cases crowns used on top of dental implants in order to create a natural looking smile.

Inlay/Onlay/Composite Fillings

You have probably noticed another person, either singing or laughing out loud with one of those big open-mouth smiles, the large, gray fillings. The fillings are actually made out of mercury, also known as amalgams, which have come under a lot of scrutiny in terms of their potential health side effects. Mercury is a toxic material, regulated by the government. You cannot safely handle it. You can't even flush it down the drain. But years ago the material was utilized for dental fillings.

It makes sense that many people now want to remove this material from their teeth! We can now replace those amalgam fillings with either a tooth-colored, resin-based filling material or with an inlay or onlay—a porcelain restoration that fits in the area where the existing filling was and is made to match the existing teeth. Inlays and onlays made of porcelain are options that will provide a little bit more durability and are often more aesthetically pleasing than a composite filling.

Yet another option for replacing a missing or discolored mercury filling is to have a crown on the tooth. Sometimes the existing filling is so large and has caused so much damage to the teeth, then the only option that you have really is to go with a crown.

Cosmetic Bonding

Cosmetic bonding is using composite resin material to make minor corrections in the tooth, to close gaps or spaces, to cover up a small stain, or to resurface the tooth like we would with the veneers. Composite can be used to veneer the tooth, repair a chipped tooth, or to fill a spot where you have a cavity.

Cosmetic bonding is probably one of the more economical ways of achieving a nice cosmetic improvement, but it's also the least durable method. It can be subject to staining and also the surface gloss or texture of the composite can be altered over time more readily than a porcelain restoration, veneer or a crown.

A primary benefit of cosmetic bonding is that it can be accomplished in one sitting, chair-side, whereas the veneers and the crowns typically are a multiple-visit type of restoration, requiring temporary restorations while the final restoration is being made.

Surgical

For some patients, dental surgery is the best option for a beautiful, healthy smile. You've probably seen people with a severe underbite or a severe overbite. Those conditions can only be corrected by making changes in the skeletal structure of the upper or lower jaw. Beginning this type of treatment requires a combination of input from your dentist, potentially an orthodontist, and an oral surgeon in order to make those corrections.

Surgically repositioning the upper or lower jaw to have a more favorable position not only pays big dividends in how your smile is improved but also can create major improvements in the function of your teeth, the long-term health of your jaw joint, and your entire chewing system.

Dentures

The denture was the original cosmetic procedure in dentistry. Years ago, when people began to lose their teeth, had decay, or just had a problematic smile, the only way to fix the issue was to have a pair of dentures made. You could create any kind of teeth or look with a pair of dentures; all of the original cosmetic dental principles were developed with denture wearers in mind.

Dentures can make a huge difference in somebody's smile. For patients who have bite-related problems, bone loss, or if they have teeth that not visible when smiling, dentures can be truly transformational. They can take someone who looks 70 or 80 years old and make them look 40 years old. It's amazing how many years having a well-made, well-fitted denture can take off of somebody's life. Dentures can be an extremely aesthetic, extremely powerful tool to improve somebody's self-image and quality of life.

Today, the use of dentures is made even more effective, because we're often connecting these dentures to dental implants, making them more stable and secure. That additional stability gives denture wearers the confidence of knowing they can be themselves in any kind of social environment without the fear of the denture flopping out.

TMJ

When it hurts to smile, TMJ may be the culprit. This condition can be truly debilitating, affecting not only the ability to smile, but the entire personality. People suffering with pain often are in no mood to smile and have to deal with these types of chronic issues. Solving TMJ problems can restore a person's ability and desire to smile, because they are free from pain and have a new lease on life.

I encourage people, even those who are experiencing minor symptoms of TMJ such as popping, clicking of the joint, ringing in the ear, head and neck pain, frequent headaches, to seek attention from a well-qualified dentist who knows a lot about TMJ to prevent it from being a hindrance in the smile.

Gum Surgery

Gum surgery enters the picture as a smile benefit when a patient has short teeth and a smile in which too much of the gums are exposed, creating a "gummy smile." When the person smiles and the lip line goes way up and you see a whole lot of gum, that's typically a very unattractive look. In some cases, gum surgery can lift the level of the gums in order to expose more teeth and less gum.

In some cases, the problem requires more than gum surgery. An additional surgical procedure is necessary to alleviate the gummy smile. Another option is to change the way the lip lies over the smile, for example, through procedures like Botox, which can be used to paralyze some of the elevator muscles in the smile in order to limit how far the upper lip goes during a smile.

One gum surgical procedure option involves removing some of the tissue where the gum and lip come together in an area called the vestibule. Removing tissue in this area pulls the lip down so it does not rise as much during the smile.

How to Improve Your Lips

While we often think of the teeth as being the most significant component of the smile, the lips play a very powerful role. If the lips are not right, the entire smile can be off and have less impact or inhibit proper communication of our feelings and emotions.

More and more people, from business men and women to celebrities, are experiencing the powerful impact lip improvement can have on the smile and how they want to communicate to those around them. Lips create a smile, a kiss, a frown and can be the determining factor as to whether we look youthful or aged.

If teeth are the actors in the role of the smile, lips are like the curtains—they frame the smile. For this reason, it is important to consider the lips when trying to create the ideal smile. Certain celebrities are well-known for their full lips, which give them a desirable image. Beautiful lips are typically characterized by:

- Healthy volume

- The right contours

- Well balanced and proportioned

There are many different ways to augment one's lips to create a beautiful smile, which will in turn enhance self-image and self-confidence. The right procedures can take thin, aged, ill-proportioned lips to fuller, aesthetically-pleasing and smile-enhancing, youthful lips.

From a nonsurgical standpoint, one of the most popular lip augmentation techniques involves fillers:

- Radiesse® is an FDA-approved calcium-based filler that lasts an average of two years.

- Restylane® and Juvederm® are hyaluronic acid fillers. Hyaluronic acid is an injectable gel that is naturally found in the body. It is easy to inject with a low chance of rejection and is absorbed over time. While it is a temporary procedure, it lasts quite a while and provides quick and simple changes to the lips.

For example, if you were someone who had a really thin upper lip that wasn't proportioned or didn't match properly with your lower lip, you would be able to augment that lip in order to make it fuller so it would match better with your lower lip.

Some patients complain of having a lot of wrinkles or lines around their lips. These lines are called perioral wrinkles. Often a result of smoking, the perioral wrinkles can be filled with dermal fillers to improve the smile and create a more youthful, healthy look.

If you think dermal fillers are right for you, it is important to know exactly what type of look you want to achieve with the treatment. We've also seen those people who go over the top with lip augmentation and have to live with platypus or duckbill-like lips that are obviously very unnatural. Surprisingly enough, some patients desire that look, but most prefer a natural, attractive lip look that is more subtle. Talk with your doctor to ensure he or she knows what your goal is, so you can be pleased with the results.

For surgical lip augmentations, there are lip implants, such as the VeraFil implant or saline implants. The surgical implants are more stable than the injectable hyaluronic acid, but over time will need to be replaced.

There are some surgical techniques, such as the V-Y Technique, available using no implants or fillers, instead using incisions to adjust the tissue in the upper and lower lips. This is permanent, and the results are subtle.

Over-the-counter lip plumpers seem to have varying effects. While some may provide slight plumping, they do not provide the significant results available through injectable or surgical techniques. I tend to recommend injectables over surgery for most patients, because with the injectable gel the material will reabsorb into the body and the lips with go back to normal in time. Whereas with a surgical procedure, you are stuck with the results, and it is difficult to hide your lips if you happen to have undesirable results.

Botox is another option for enhancing your lips. It works by paralyzing certain muscles, and when it comes to lips Botox can paralyze the depressor muscles that tend to pull-down at the corner of your lips. This then allows the elevating muscle to pull up the corner of the lips, improving the smile.

Maximizing Your Smile as a Whole

We've covered your options for enhancing and improving the individual components of your smile, which leaves us to address the entire smile as a whole. How do you improve your smile in your own strength and ability and know when to use the proper smile in the right situation? It all comes down to three actions:

1. Look at yourself in the mirror.

2. Know what the ideal smile looks like.

3. Understand what that smile feels like on your face, so you can know how to replicate it.

Think of it this way—one of things that make professional athletes so successful is muscle memory. A golfer must remember the exact feel of that exact swing in order to pull off that perfect shot. Basketball players develop just the right touch, the way the ball feels in their fingertips, in order to make that free throw or jump shot.

Can you see how it is the same way with you and your ideal smile? If you don't practice, if you don't develop the muscle memory for the ideal smile, you never know if you're actually pulling off the ideal smile when it counts the most.

A great example of this in the acting industry is Jim Carrey. He is a master of facial expression. He has been interviewed before and spends a lot of time practicing his facial expressions in the mirror and developing a muscle memory on how that expression feels. Because of this "practice," he knows how to replicate certain facial expressions to achieve certain effects.

When it comes to our smiles, we must develop the strength in our musculature to be able to smile in the ideal way. We can actually do smile exercises to develop the proper muscles you will need to use in your smiling. Check out this simple exercise below designed to strengthen your smile muscles:

Let start off with some smile stretches to loosen up those muscles before we start our smile workout.

Smile Stretches

Bubble Stretches

The bubble stretch is very easy. Close your lips and blow a bubble and inflate your right cheek, move to left cheek then upper lip and lower, hold each for approximately 10 – 12 seconds. And complete 5 reps. You will feel a really good stretch as you inflate those smile muscles.

Max Opening Stretches

Open your mouth as wide as you can and hold for 5 second count then relax. Repeat this stretch about 8 – 10 times. If you have TMJ problems or are prone to lock jaw you may want to avoid this stretch.

Smile Exercises

The Lip Press

Press your lips together like you're puckering up for a kiss; hold then fill your cheek with air while holding the lips together for 8 seconds. Do 5 reps of this exercise.

O Pull

Make an oval with an "O" shape with your mouth, with your lips apart. Hold that position while attempting to smile. You will feel your cheek muscles flexing. Hold for 5 seconds and do 5 reps of this exercise.

Balance Stick

Place a pencil or a chopstick between your front teeth and smile so that no part of your lips touch the stick. Hold for 10 seconds and do 5 reps of this exercise. 5 reps works great to help create a full smile.

Lip Extensions

This exercise is not easy and may take some practice to perform but it's a great exercise to help maintain the tone and help with fullness of upper lip. Start by extending the upper lip into a pucker and pout position and hold for 10 seconds. The goal is to try to touch your nose with your upper lip while allowing your lip to curve up or rotate and with some practice you should be able to do this. Repeat this exercise 3 times.

Lip Extensions with Dumbbell

Repeat the lip extensions exercise but use a pencil and try to hold it in place between the lip and nose. Hold this position for 8 seconds, relax and repeat for 3 sets.

Cheek Press

To do this exercise correctly you must create a small "O" with your lips. Then press or squeeze the cheeks together forming a pucker. Try not to engage the lip muscles but use the cheeks muscles to push the lips together. This will take some carefully focus to engage the correct muscles. Hold each press for 8 seconds. Relax and repeat 3 times.

Smile Push Up

1. Start by forming a big smile. Hold this smile while placing fingers about a quarter inch from each corner of your smile.

2. With moderate pressure from your fingers retract the smile half way against the finger pressure and hold for 8 seconds.

3. Close you smile all the way until your lips touch. Maintain constant from your finger and hold for 10 seconds. Relax.

4. Now let reverse the process. Place your finger in the same position without a smile.

5. Hold the finger pressure and move to a half smile. Hold for 8 – 10 seconds.

6. Lower the finger pressure and push out to smile and hold for 10 seconds and relax.

7. Complete 3 reps.

Smile Aerobics For Emotional Health[102]

One way to become better at smiling is increasing your awareness. Take notice of those you find warm and inviting. Is it their smile? Make an effort to LOOK for great smiles. Notice the appeal of people who smile with their EYES, not just their mouth. The whole face gets involved. Consider these people your models. Study yourself in the mirror. How do you look in the rest room, when shopping, and while passing a reflective window? Do you look friendly? Approachable? Do you really LIKE the image you're projecting?

In fact, a mirror is ideal for your smile workout. Practice various smiles toward capturing that perfect look for the camera. Work on expressing your smile with your eyes. A tip: cut a paper rectangle that permits you to see only your eyes in the mirror. Practice smiling just with your eyes. Get used to the feel of your cheekbones as they lift to brighten your eyes. When you see how a great smile LOOKS, remember how it FEELS. When you can finally project your best smile, hold it. Turn away from the mirror. How does your face feel? What muscles are you using? Make an effort to develop muscle memory, so you can instantly recreate this smile at will.

We've also covered the importance of using your eyes appropriately when smiling, so you will want to practice and memorize the correct way to use your eyes in smiling. Back in 2009, model and talk show host Tyra Banks made the news for coining a new phrase called "smizing," in which a person learns to smile with only his or her eyes.[103]

While it was spoofed on many late night talk shows, there was really something to her idea of smizing. There is great power within the eyes, so it is important to harness this power as your train yourself to discover and fine-tune your ideal smile.

Improve Your Life = Improve Your Smile

The way to achieve a naturally beautiful smile is to find and experience true happiness. People who are happy inside have a tendency to smile more. In Chapter 5, we addressed the psychological aspects of smiling, and how a smile can actually create more happiness in our lives—like a Domino effect.

It all boils down to having a balanced lifestyle, being at peace with yourself, and being at peace with others. People who have a happy, balanced lifestyle are typically the people who you will find walking around with a smile upon their faces. We aren't talking about a fake smile but rather a genuine Duchenne smile that warms-up the entire face and makes people who encounter the smile feel good.

Smiling, like laughter, increases those feel-good endorphins in your brain, so practicing the act of smiling as often as you can will give your mood a boost. The amazing power of the smile goes something like this:

1. You make a choice to smile.

2. You do the action of smiling.

3. You set off the endorphins and your mood is improved.

4. You create a chain-reaction of smiling; you smile at someone and they smile back at you, increasing their own endorphins.

5. The more you reinforce this process, the more and more it becomes a natural part of your lifestyle.

If you find yourself in a rut in which you don't feel like smiling, give yourself a pep talk. Remind yourself of the numerous benefits of smiling and how it can greatly enhance your life and the lives of those people around you.

The self-help philosophy called Psycho-Cybernetics, coined by author and cosmetic surgeon Maxwell Maltz, addresses how important the perspective and mind are in achieving personal satisfaction with appearance and in life. He found that unless his cosmetic surgery patients altered the way they thought about themselves, their behaviors after the surgery were often the same as they were prior to the surgery. For example, they would have similar avoidance patterns and compensatory behaviors for perceived shortcomings. It was as if nothing had changed about their bodies, because their mind had remained unchanged.

Until they were able to accept themselves psychologically and change the way they thought about themselves, the behavior didn't change.

What does this mean for you? Let's say you obtain Invisalign or you have your smile altered in some way. Until you really accept yourself and change unhealthy behavior you've been so accustomed to—hiding your smile, feeling embarrassed of your smile, or not smiling at all—you might not be able to fully embrace or utilize your new smile. To reap the full benefits of your new smile, you must understand what the current reality is, not what the former reality was, and then behave accordingly.

It's safe to say that achieving your ideal smile is much more than a simple dental procedure or lip augmentation. The process must involve the mind and the way you see yourself and the world around you. When you can strive to transform your mind as you physically transform your smile, you will be able to experience the life-changing impact of a natural, healthy smile in many different areas of your life.

Smile Stories… Dental Fear Conquered

I had several cavities on front teeth. I was ashamed to laugh. I'm very afraid of the dentist and that was the main reason why I didn't fix my teeth. Because I found on out on the Internet that there is potential to get seriously ill from rotting teeth, I gathered courage and some money and went to my friend, who began working in private practice as a dentist. The job was finished in two days. During the repair I asked the dentist to explain the whole process of fixing teeth; it was a way to overcome my fear, because I knew I was doing something good for me and my dental health.

After that, I no longer felt ashamed of my smile and I was pleased with how my teeth looked and felt. Since then, I've gone to the dentist regularly and maintain my teeth carefully. I can only say that my life has changed a lot and especially my confidence level. My friends were amazed by the appearance of my teeth. Until then, they had not commented because they didn't want to embarrass me. So I can say that I now have a smile that is a favorite among my friends and that's nice.

Smile Stories... No More Hiding

I used to always duck my head in public, lacking the confidence I needed to look people in the eyes. I'd also be disinclined to smile, especially if it meant opening my mouth. I was constantly hiding my mouth with my hand and confided how people often thought I was stupid, drug addicted or lazy because I was lacking front teeth.

I never cared for apples or corn on the cob and still can't eat them. My front teeth partial dentures were mainly for looks, although I said it also helps to bite off portions of softer foods. Instead of cramming a sandwich into the back part of my mouth, I can now eat like a normal person, biting with my front teeth.

While I am too embarrassed to take out the front teeth partial denture plate to show anyone, I described what it's like. I have a row of four teeth to replace those that are missing. The teeth are connected to a plate, which fits snugly on the roof of my mouth. The sides of the plate have little clasps that hook around the molars so the front teeth partial dentures stay in place. My favorite features of the denture plate are that the color matches the rest of her teeth and no clasps are visible from the front. They look so real.

Smile Stories... Now I Can Eat What I Want

I had a very painful tooth that prevented me from eating certain foods. I consulted with the dentist and was informed that he could save the tooth with a root canal. Before the root canal, my tooth was very sensitive to heat and cold. It was difficult for me to eat things like ice cream or a popsicle without pain. Eating sweets was also at times difficult for me. The pain would also be present at various times with or without food in my mouth.

It took a while after the root canal for the pain to completely go away. But after several months I was finally able to eat the foods that I was reluctant to eat due to the impending discomfort I would have to endure. I have another tooth on the other side of mouth that needs a root canal and I would not hesitate to have the procedure done again to stop the pain and to be able to enjoy the foods that I like to eat.

Next

Now that we've looked at specific ways to improve your smile, let's take a look at all that we've learned and take action on it.

Chapter 10

Smile Success: Putting it all Together

Smile at what used to be
The glory and the agony
Smile at a memory
Smile at your enemies
A smile finally saved me, found me and repaid me
For all the time that I've put in
And now I'm smiling back again
Just smile for a while
We've just begun to smile
Smile for a while
"A Smile," Lyrics by Hootie and the Blowfish

Throughout this book, it has been our goal to reveal to you the power of smiling and the great impact it can have on numerous aspects of your life. Furthermore, we have covered the options available to you as you strive to achieve your ideal smile, so you can use your smile to your advantage in your personal and professional life.

Because we have covered so much ground in the previous ten chapters, this final chapter will provide you with a condensed version of the highlights of each chapter accompanied by action steps you can take today to begin maximizing your smile. As we've discussed before, knowledge is power but taking action is transformational, so we encourage you to run with the information you have learned through this book.

Chapter Highlights

Preface: Beginning the Journey to a Beautiful Smile

It is here where we began your journey to a beautiful, effective smile that gives you an advantage in all different aspects of your life. We provided a quick overview of each chapter as well as smile stories to inspire and motivate you.

Action Step for the Preface

- Open your mind and imagine all of the possibilities and opportunities that await you when you can begin to achieve and utilize your ideal smile.

Chapter 1: Why Should You Smile More?

From improved health and stress reduction to more harmonious relationships and workplace success, the benefits of smiling are numerous. Study after study and researcher after researcher have revealed how influential the smile can be in the quality, healthfulness and longevity of our daily lives.

In Chapter 1, we covered five health-related benefits of smiling:

1. Stress Relief
2. Strengthening of the Immune System
3. Decreasing Blood Pressure
4. Releasing Endorphins, Natural Pain Killers and Serotonin
5. Lifting the Face and Providing a More Youthful Look

When it comes to familial relationships, children and adults alike respond positively to smiling. A household void of smiling tends to be much less positive and more troubled overall. In fact, a house where frowning or lack of smiling is prevalent, negativity and discouragement tend to be the overriding emotions.

A smile provides the following benefits in familial relationships:

- Communicates unconditional love.
- Creates a positive atmosphere in the home.
- Helps family members feel valued, welcomed and appreciated.

For those individuals who are interested in attracting a love interest, a smile can be their secret weapon. When you stop to consider people whom you find attractive, it is very likely that they have a nice smile. It is rare that we find people who do not smile attractive. That goes to show just how important a smile can be if you are looking for a fun date or a serious relationship.

A smile works as a magnet, drawing people to you and causing them to be interested. People enjoy being around people who smile. Plus, the smile creates that Domino effect where others begin to smile back at you and the entire environment, whether it is the grocery store or a club, is changed for the better.

It is helpful to consider the magnetic power of the smile when using dating websites. Always choose a profile photo that displays a beautiful smile. Forget the duck lips and pouts; a smile is what will get another person's attention—the right kind of attention, that is.

In addition to personal relationships, a smile is one of the most effective tools you have to achieve success in the workplace. Smiling makes you attractive to all people, including your potential boss in an interview, or the people considering you for a promotion. It makes you seem more friendly and confident, which in turn makes you seem like a good candidate or leader.

A smile gives the impression that you are a team player and would make a good representative for your company. It also helps you to work better on the job through building rapport with co-workers and customers, providing friendly customer service, and earning positive reviews from managers and other people in the workplace.

Chapter 1 Action Steps
- Remind yourself of the benefits of smiling often.
- If smiling is a challenge for you, write a list of benefits smiling has for your unique situation on a notecard. Paste the notecard somewhere you can see it often—on your mirror in the bathroom, at your desk at work, or on the dashboard of your car.
- Remember that your smile sets off a Domino effect of smiling. If you set the cycle in motion, people will smile back at you. In this way, you can break the ice and warm up any environment or situation with your smile.

Chapter 2: How Smiling Increase Your Business Success

The idea that it is best to have a stern, hard appearance to prove yourself as a leader in the workplace is no longer relevant. In our culture today, the smile is much more likely to earn the respect and attention of co-workers and bosses alike. Whether you are trying to land a job, hoping for a promotion, or want to succeed as a leader, your smile is your most effective tool to get there.

Because the first impression is so important when it comes to job interviews, it is essential to remember to smile. In fact, the smile is the focal point during a first impression. Make the most of your smile with good oral hygiene and dental care.

Researchers have found that appearance can be even more important than qualifications when it comes to the workplace. Studies have revealed that people who are viewed as attractive are more likely to achieve success in their careers. We know a smile makes you more attractive, so it is safe to say that you really shouldn't go to an interview or work without it.

Smiling also makes you a more valuable employee—particularly in the field of customer service. Your customers will feel more valued, and it will be easier to establish good rapport with them if you smile often. Even if your customer service is over the phone, the customers can actually hear your smile.

If you are in a role of leadership or hope to be one day, a smile helps you to create a positive environment in the office that is conducive to team work and increased productivity. Coworkers or employees are much more likely to enjoy working for you and do the best job possible when you smile as you interact with them.

Chapter 2 Action Steps:

- Just as you prepare yourself for potential interview questions and get your suit ready, you want to prepare your smile for job interviews.

- Practice the smile you want to use in the office or in interviews, so you can become comfortable using it.

- Forget about old fashioned ideas that being stern with a face of stone is a good business move. You can build rapport with co-workers and customers as well as create a warmer and more productive work environment when you give your smile freely.

Chapter 3: How Smiling Improves Your Social Life

In Chapter 3, we touched on the importance of the first impression in business scenarios, but the smile plays a very important role in the first impression for social scenarios as well. In a few brief seconds, another person meeting you for the first time takes an assessment and makes a judgment based on what they see.

While some may believe it's the hairstyle or clothing or body shape that creates the first impression, the reality is that the smile, or lack of smile, garners the most attention. People look directly at your face in the moment of the first impression, and they base their assessment on what they see in your facial expression. All of this takes place on a subconscious level.

This is why it is so important to use your smile to your advantage in social situations, particularly when you are meeting people for the first time. Your smile paves the way for a warm, open, friendly and confident impression. Isn't that the kind of impression you want to make on others?

By using your smile, you can become much more approachable. Couple your smile with appropriate eye contact and you have a major social advantage. An interesting statistic in this chapter revealed that 90% of men said they would not approach a woman unless he sees an inviting smile. 90%! Putting a warm smile on your face while making eye contact can literally mean the difference between loneliness and romance.

While there are many different types of smiles to use in a social environment, the Duchenne smile is the most natural, ideal smile. This smile involves contraction of certain muscles around the eyes, forming crow's feet. There's something about this smile that evokes true happiness, and it is easy to see that this is not a fake or put-on smile.

The Duchenne smile increases brain activity in the part of the brain responsible for positive emotion, so using this type of smile will boost your mood and help you to feel happier, which will in turn make you even more appealing to the opposite sex.

Of course, good oral hygiene is another important factor in succeeding with your smile in social situations. There's really no way to mask bad oral hygiene, so if you are serious about maximizing your smile and using it to your advantage in social situations, address any problematic dental issues and take steps to have good oral hygiene on a daily basis.

Chapter 3 Action Steps:

- Make the best first impression possible in social situations by showing your smile.

- If you have dental problems or poor oral hygiene, address those issues to put your best smile forward with confidence.

- Discover and use your natural Duchenne smile to share a genuine smile that attracts others to you and promotes positivity.

- You don't have to look perfect or have designer clothes to attract others. Your smile is your best and most effective asset. Learn how to use it, and you can get out there in the social world with confidence.

Chapter 4: How Smiling Helps Your Mental Health

When you really dig deep into the impact of your smile, it can be surprising how much it communicates to those around you. You may not have previously realized it, but a smile sends a message about your gender, personality and psychological make-up. A smile sends messages to others without you having to speak a word.

Your teeth and the way they are displayed in your mouth also affect the impression you give to others regarding the femininity and masculinity of your appearance. Cosmetic dental procedures now make it possible for you to design a smile to help you express the traits you find most desirable.

It may be that you aren't pleased with the smile you were born with because it gives an incorrect impression of who you are. The good news is that you can do something about it with the help of a knowledgeable dentist who understands the psychological aspects of the smile and how you can use smile design to achieve desired look.

Dentists can round out pointed canine teeth to eliminate an overly-aggressive appearance, or straighten tilted lateral incisors to create a more masculine smile. There's no need to settle. The right dentist will work with you to achieve your smile goals while ensuring you maintain optimal teeth functionality.

Chapter 4 Action Steps:
- Work with a dentist who is knowledgeable when it comes to the psychological aspects of the smile and the various gender and personality traits teeth can promote.

- Identify any aspects about your teeth you wish to change and identify the message you wish to send with your smile.

- Only choose a dentist who will focus on appearance of your teeth as well as proper teeth functioning.

Chapter 5: How Smiling Makes You Healthier

While people commonly think the smile is a result of being happy, it is also true that smiling can create happiness. Even faking a smile can release hormones, neurotransmitters and endorphins in your brain that bring forth a happy feeling. You may begin with a fake smile, but once those endorphins start pumping you being to smile quite naturally.

Other physiological benefits to smiling include:

- Smiling can be a stress reducer in difficult situations.

- Smiling leads to more favorable impressions of the people around us; people are funnier, more enjoyable, more entertaining when you have a smile on your face.

- When we are smiling and laughing, new, healthy cell production increases.

- A smile elevates antibody levels in the blood and saliva, which increases immunity and improves health.

Because smiles have been shown to boost the immune system, people with chronic illness are effectively using smiling and laughter as medicine. The famous doctor Patch Adams is one person who is well known for using smiles, jokes, and laughter in healing. While humor can boost the immune system and reduce stress, it also benefits patients by taking their minds off of their illness for a time.

Chapter 5 Action Steps:
- If you don't feel like smiling, go ahead and fake it 'til you make it! Putting a smile on your face when you don't feel like it stimulates things on a physiological level in such a way that your mood will improve and you will begin to smile naturally.

- If you don't particularly enjoy the people you are with, smile anyway. Smiling can actually change your impression of them, so you find them more interesting.

- Remember than smiling can boost your immune system while reducing stress levels. If you are going through a time of illness or facing a chronic illness, or are just under a lot of stress, carve out some time in your schedule to laugh and smile. Whether it is watching a funny movie or laughing with a friend, it can benefit your health and well-being to smile.

Chapter 6: Different Smiles for Different Occasions

As unique as people are it makes sense that there are a plethora of smile types to express a wide range of emotions. While we rarely stop to consider what our smiles communicate to others, the fact remains that different types of smiles send different messages. Furthermore, some smiles are ideal for certain settings while other smiles can actually seem inappropriate.

Author and Researcher Paul Ekman provided extensive information regarding the classifications of different smile types. We can look to his research to gain a better understanding as to how we can utilize certain smiles most effectively to communicate a desired message. Having the knowledge of these different smile types and knowing how to use them will help you to create the social results you want.

Some of Ekman's categories of smiles include:

- Enjoyment Smile—such as the previously discussed Duchenne smile

- Felt Smile—smiling with the eyes only

- Enjoyment of Others—sweet, pleasant smile, enjoying the company of another person either romantically or just socially

- Happiness of Relief—comes from a place of relief, for not having to deal with a fear, threat or worry

- Pleasure from Tactile, Auditory or Visual Stimulation

- Amusement

- Contentment

- Botox—paralyzed facial muscles, unnatural smile

- Arrogant

- Confident

- Laughing

- Sexy

- Felt Smiles Blended Emotions

- Non Enjoyment Smiles

- False Smiles

Going through the smile types though this chapter can help you to gain a better understanding of what different smiles mean and the messages you communicate with them. This knowledge will benefit you as you become more aware of the messages you send with your facial expressions, but it can also help you to become more in-tune with the expressions and various communications styles of those around you.

Chapter 6 Action Steps

- As you consider the ideal smile for certain situations, ask yourself the following questions:

  - How do others perceive you when you smile?

  - What do you want to communicate when you are smiling at someone?

  - What smile is appropriate for this situation?

- Go through the list of Ekman's smile types to identify smiles that you may want to utilize in certain social situations and then begin practicing them in the mirror.

- Take a mental note of the reactions and responses you receive from those around when you are using your new smile types.

Chapter 7: What Makes Up a Smile?

Chapter 7 took a closer look at the primary components of a smile and how they can work together to create the ideal smile. A major point of the section is that it isn't just about the teeth. It is possible to have nice, shiny, white straight teeth, yet have an unattractive smile due to gum issues or unsightly lips.

The right dental care and other medical procedures will optimize each of the smile components, giving you your best chance possible at a beautiful smile design that will help you to communicate better with others.

Tooth Shape and Length

The way teeth portray gender is an important consideration as you strive to make the most of the teeth Mother Nature gave you. Square, angular teeth create a more masculine smile, while rounded teeth promote a feminine appearance. Patients can adjust their smile design to be more masculine or feminine, depending on the message they want to send with their smile.

In the same way, pointed canine teeth tend to suggest a dominant personality trait, while rounded canine teeth are associated with a more passive personality. Some patients may believe that their career or social life will benefit from a more masculine, feminine, dominant or passive look, so they can work with a dentist who is experienced in how teeth portray gender and personality to achieve their smile design goals.

Porcelain veneers or crowns are often good options for patients who want to focus on creating the ideal tooth length to complement their unique face shape and look.

Lips

While not as often considered, lips play a major role in the beauty and effectiveness of a smile. The send certain messages and suggest personality traits that may or may not line up with your true personality.

Lips are highly expressive and contribute to the overall look of the smile and the facial features. The size of the lips as well as equilibrium, shape and lip line determine how much of the teeth and gums are exposed and greatly impact the smile as a whole.

Gums

Gums can also send non-verbal messages to those around us, and they deserve the proper attention as significant components of smile design. Some common concerns you may have with your gums that need to be addressed by a professional include:

- Excessive gingival exposure
- Uneven gum contours
- Inflammation
- Exposure of root surfaces

Each of these problems can detract from the smile's beauty and message, but a dentist can work with you to create a treatment plan to make the most of the gums you possess.

In many cases, you may find that the smile you received at birth does not line up with the personality traits you wish to communicate to others, but cosmetic dentistry provides options for you to obtain the look that will help you to fine-tune the non-verbal messages your smile components send out into the world.

Chapter 7 Action Steps:
- Understand that the impact of your smile depends upon more than just your teeth. In order to maximize your smile design, consider all components of the smile.
- Find a dentist who will address each of the smile components.
- Determine what personality traits and messages you wish to share with the world through your smile and then enhance your teeth, lips and gums to better communicate those.
- Never fear if the smile Mother Nature gave you doesn't line up with your personality; the right dental work can get you on track.

Chapter 8: How Smiling Helps Kids and Teens

Chapter 8 covered the reasons how the smile can impact the quality of life for kids and teens. From the first days of a human beings life, they respond to and learn about smiling from those around them, and this interaction shapes who they will become and how they will one day use their smile to communicate to others.

Parents can begin to model good dental hygiene and dental care to children early, but they can also impart unconditional love and nurturing to their children through frequently sharing their smile with them.

An infant's experience with smiling in the early developmental stages directly impacts his or her smiles as a child and teen. It is typically the teen years when more problems and social issues develop in regards to the smile.

Children and teens who feel confident in their smiles are better able to handle life's challenges, meet new people and provide a positive impression to those around them, which will benefit them throughout their lives.

A healthy smile is a teen's best asset. It does more than just reflect kindness to others, it providers the smiler with increased confidence and gives them an emotional boost, so they feel better about themselves and their outlook on life improves.

A smile has the power to set off a cycle of friendliness, self-acceptance, acceptance of others, and sharing positive feelings with others—all important to the life of a child or teen. It is the parent's job to help them learn how to participate in this cycle.

If they feel ashamed of their teeth, it may be difficult for them to utilize the smile effectively in relating with others. As parents and caregivers, we can encourage them to take the necessary steps to have a healthy smile that begins with the foundation of good dental hygiene and care.

- Flossing regularly
- Regular dentist visits to deal with cavities and other dental issues that can impact their best smiles possible
- Teeth straightening procedures
- Whitening treatments—professional in-office treatment is safest and most effective

Because children and teens have busy, active lives and often do not give a second thought to the health of their teeth, it is the caregiver's responsibility to teach them about good oral hygiene as well as model it to them. Furthermore, guiding children and teens to achieve healthy self-esteems and positive self-images will enable them to optimize the use of their smiles to make the most of it now and throughout their lives.

Chapter 8 Action Steps:

- Be aware of the fact that as parents and caregivers we have the honor of modeling good oral hygiene and dental care as well as showing children unconditional love through smiles.

- Addressing dental problems for children and teens will help them to have greater confidence in their smiles, so they will want to use them more often. Find a dentist who specializes in care for children and teens to set them up for success.

- Ensure children know exactly what they should be doing to keep their smile healthy with regular dental care they can do at home, and also provide them options for teeth straightening and whitening when necessary.

Chapter 9: How to Improve Your Smile

In Chapter 9, we covered in detail the many dental options available to you, including:

- Invisalign/Traditional Braces
- Veneers
- Whitening
- Tooth Replacement
- Crowns
- Inlay/Onlay/Composite Fillings
- Cosmetic Bonding
- Surgical

- Dentures

- TMJ

- Gum Surgery

- Lip Augmentation

Practicing Your Smile

In addition to receiving the right type of dental care and procedure, smile practice is a way to improve your smile in your own strength, on you own time—no dentist required. This smile practice goes something like this:

- Look at yourself in the mirror.

- Know what the ideal smile looks like.

- Understand what that smile feels like on your face, so you can know how to replicate it.

Strive for a Happy, Balanced Life

All of the dental procedures and smile practice in the world can only go so far in creating a beautiful smile. The truth is that finding and experiencing true happiness in life is what brings out the most genuine and lovely smile. It's all about being at peace with yourself and with others. The people who can obtain this place of peace are the ones who tend to walk around with a smile upon their face most of the day.

Chapter 9 Action Steps
- Take the Smile Self-Analysis to assess the characteristics of your teeth, the messages they communicate, and how your current teeth and smile line up with what you desire for your appearance and communication.

- Use the results from these two pieces to determine what dental procedures you may utilize to maximize your smile and be prepared with information regarding those procedures to discuss with your dentist.

- Keep in mind that a balanced, peaceful life is the best source of your most beautiful smile.

Appendix

1 Restored Church of God (RCG). (2003). Smile! Retrieved from http://rcg.org/youth/articles/0101-s.html

2 Kuenne, K. (Writer) (2008). "validation"-the power of a smile [Web]. Retrieved from http://www.youtube.com/watch?v=IRE5os7wQeI

3 Gutman, R. (2011, May). The hidden power of smiling [Video file]. Retrieved from http://www.ted.com/talks/ron_gutman_the_hidden_power_of_smiling.html

4 Gutman, R. (2011, May). The hidden power of smiling [Video file]. Retrieved from http://www.ted.com/talks/ron_gutman_the_hidden_power_of_smiling.html

5 Stibich, M. (2010, February 4). Top 10 Reasons to Smile. About.com. Retrieved March 2011, from http://longevity.about.com/od/lifelongbeauty/tp/smiling.htm

6 Star, E. S. (2009). Smile!the secret science of smiling. Asheville, NC: Roaring Lion Publishing, Inc.

7 Gutman, R. (2011, May). The hidden power of smiling [Video file]. Retrieved from http://www.ted.com/talks/ron_gutman_the_hidden_power_of_smiling.html

8 Restored Church of God (RCG). (2003). Smile! Retrieved from http://rcg.org/youth/articles/0101-s.html

9 Expertvillage (2007, October 3). How to Win Beauty Pageants : Keeping a Winning Smile During a Beauty Pageant [Video File]. Retrieved from http://www.youtube.com/watch?v=ok7p2k6jo28

10 Carnegie, D. (2009). In How to win friends and influence people (p. 320). New York, USA: Simon & Schuster.

11 Martin, C. (2010, November 29). Why Is Your Smile the Universal Communicator? The Science May Surprise You, Says Richmond Cosmetic Dentist - Press Release. Press Release Distribution | Press Release Distribution Services. Retrieved July 3, 2011, from http://www.ereleases.com/pr/smile-universal-communicator-science-surprise-richmond-cosmetic-dentist-43432

12 Stanger, M. (2012, October 11). Attractive people see greater success at work
    - Money - TODAY.com. TODAY - Top News Stories, Video Clips, Recipes and
    Guests | TODAY.com. Retrieved November 24, 2012, from http://www.today.
    com/id/49350507/site/todayshow/ns/today-money/t/hey-good-lookin-your-job-
    outlook-lookin-good/#.UIljAoZ8byU

13 Spector, P.E. (2007) Industrial and organizational psychology, research and
    practice (5 ed.), Wiley

14 Richardson, N. M. (2010, April 30). 10 Ways the CEO Can Reduce Office Stress |
    Inc.com.Small Business Ideas and Resources for Entrepreneurs. Retrieved March
    25, 2011, from http://www.inc.com/guides/2010/04/reduce-office-stress.html

15 Beall Research & Training of Chicago. (2004). Can a new smile make you appear
    more successful and intelligent?. Consumer Studies, Retrieved from www.aacd.
    com/proxy.php?filename=files/Footer Nav/...doc

16 CNN/Money. (2005, April 11). Surprise! Pretty people earn more money.
    CNNMoney. Retrieved from http://money.cnn.com/2005/04/08/news/funny/
    beautiful_money/

17 University of Portsmouth (2008, January 16). Smile -- And The World Can Hear
    You, Even If You Hide. ScienceDaily. Retrieved January 17, 2013, from http://
    www.sciencedaily.com¬/releases/2008/01/080111224745.htm

18 Blount, J. (2010). In People buy you: The real secret to what matters most in
    business. Hoboken, N.J: John Wiley.

19 Barger, P. B., & Grandey, A. A. (2006). service with a smile and encounter
    satisfaction: emotional contagion and appraisal mechanisms. Academy of
    Management Journal,49(6), 1229. doi:23478695

20 Barger, P. B., & Grandey, A. A. (2006). service with a smile and encounter
    satisfaction: emotional contagion and appraisal mechanisms. Academy of
    Management Journal,49(6), 1229. doi:23478695

21 Steele, J. (n.d.). Smile, Really Smile, It's Good for Health and Good for Business.
    Ezine articles. Retrieved June 10, 2011, from http://ezinearticles.com/?Smile,-
    Really-Smile,-Its-Good-for-Health-and-Good-for-Business&id=197930

22 Wood, P. (n.d.). smile through the tears- fake smiles vs. real smiles. Patti
    Wood. Retrieved April 14, 2011, from http://www.pattiwood.net/uploads/
    smilingthroughthetears.pdf

23 Greatawakening (2010, August 29). Life Coach: Smile to Feel Better [Video File].
    Retrieved from http://www.youtube.com/watch?v=OL4vIFJsIEU

24   Joyousexpansion (2011, March 6). Spiritual Life Coaching Tip: Smile More [Video File]. Retrieved from http://www.youtube.com/watch?v=37m_7jVf4bo

25   In59seconds (2009, August 11). Science of happiness: Power of Smiling [Video File]. Retrieved from http://www.youtube.com/watch?v=6SjOGO1tRXU

26   Horn, S. (1997). In Concrete confidence: A 30-day program for an unshakable foundation of self-assurance (1st ed.). New York: St. Martin's Press.

27   Wood, P. (n.d.). From Wallflower to Social Butterfly. Body Language Expert and Speaker | Patti Wood, MA, CSP. Retrieved June 12, 2011, from http://www.pattiwood.net/article.asp?PageID=8172

28   Kommersant (2006, December 18). Sharapova's Smile Called World's Best. Kommersant: Russia's Daily Online [Moscow].

29   Ellsberg, M. (2010). In The power of eye contact: Your secret for success in business, love, and life. New York: HarperPaperbacks.

30   Manly, R. (n.d.). Go Ahead and Smile. California State University, Long Beach. Retrieved March 12, 2011, from http://www.csulb.edu/misc/inside/archives/v59n1/1.htm

31   University of Texas at Austin (2010, September 26). Men look for good bodies in short-term mates, pretty faces in long-term mates.ScienceDaily. Retrieved January 21, 2013, from http://www.sciencedaily.com¬/releases/2010/09/100925105837.htm

32   Arino, B. (2010, April 11). Basic Emotions (LIE TO ME) [Video File]. Retrieved from http://www.youtube.com/watch?v=LHraznv4pHQ&feature=related

33   Tuttle, C. (2010, February 10). What Your Smile Says About Who You Are! [Video File]. Retrieved from http://www.youtube.com/watch?v=yNusttI9MyU

34   Humintell (2009, November 20). Dr. David Matsumoto, Happiness Conference explains Duchenne Smiles [Video File]. Retrieved from http://www.youtube.com/watch?v=y3_bk9jHXrI

35   Leff, B. (2007, December 1). Why Do We Smile? The Jewish Website - aish.com. Retrieved October 10, 2011, from http://www.aish.com/sp/pg/48929682.html

36   Hill, D. (2010). In About face: The secrets of emotionally effective advertising. London: Kogan Page.

37   Ask.com (n.d.). Duchenne smile | Ask.com Encyclopedia. Ask.com - What's Your Question?. Retrieved March 10, 2011, from http://www.ask.com/wiki/Duchenne_smile

38 SunStar, E. (2009). In Smile!: Your key to inner and outer radiance. Asheville, NC: Roaring Lion Pub.

39 Star (2006), shares five things your smile tells others about you:…

40 Kyoko (n.d.). If one person smiles. | Kyoko has a blog [Web log post]. Retrieved from http://thephobia.com/post/1344790780/if-one-person-smiles

41 Nettle, D. (2005). In Happiness: The science behind your smile. Oxford, UK: Oxford University Press.

42 Gero, J. (n.d.). Stress-Our Modern Dilemma.

43 Dpgplc (2010, December 19). Lie to Me - Reading Emotions and Deceit through Facial Expressions [Video File]. Retrieved from http://www.youtube.com/watch?v=RnwdndsspTI&feature=related

44 SunStar, E. (2009). In Smile!: Your key to inner and outer radiance. Asheville, NC: Roaring Lion Pub.

45 Wood, P. (n.d.). smile through the tears- fake smiles vs. real smiles. Patti Wood. Retrieved April 14, 2011, from http://www.pattiwood.net/uploads/smilingthroughthetears.pdf

46 Houlker, J., Rickaby, M., & Standeven, G. (2009). In Choosing to smile. Chilliwack, BC: Choosing to Smile Publications.

47 Doskoch, P. (1996, July 1). Happily Ever Laughter | Psychology Today. Psychology Today: Health, Help, Happiness + Find a Therapist. Retrieved June 5, 2011, from http://www.psychologytoday.com/articles/199607/happily-ever-laughter

48 Jewell, M. (2008, February 8). Shop 'til you smile. Pittsburgh Post-Gazette [Pitssburgh].

49 Sixwise.com (n.d.). Smile! The Remarkable Personal Benefits of Smiling. Healthy Family - Health and Wealth, Home Safety, Health, Relationship, Growing Family. Retrieved March 12, 2011, from http://www.sixwise.com/newsletters/05/04/12/smile-the-remarkable-personal-benefits-of-smiling.htm

50 Pitstop (2010, November 10). Social Smile - an Interesting Comparison! Bukisa - Share Your Knowledge. Retrieved January 21, 2013, from http://www.bukisa.com/articles/392378_social-smile-an-interesting-comparison#ixzz1ICq9pXOm

51 SunStar, E. (2009). In Smile!: Your key to inner and outer radiance. Asheville, NC: Roaring Lion Pub.

52 Patch Adams' Speaking (n.d.). Patch Adams' Speaking Website - Home-1. Patch Adams' Speaking Website - Home-1. Retrieved January 21, 2013, from http://www.patchadamsspeaks.com/index.html#/patchadams-bioslideshow/

53 Bernstein, D. R. (2011, June 7). The Healing Smile And How To Use It. Acupuncture in Dumbo, New York | Hypnosis Brooklyn | Acupuncturist in Brooklyn NY | Weight Loss NYC and Dumbo. Retrieved January 21, 2013, from http://bluephoenixwellness.com/the-healing-smile-and-how-to-use-it

54 SunStar, E. (2009). In Smile!: Your key to inner and outer radiance. Asheville, NC: Roaring Lion Pub.

55 SunStar, E. (2009). In Smile!: Your key to inner and outer radiance. Asheville, NC: Roaring Lion Pub.

56 Henrie M. Treadwell and Allan J. Formicola. Improving the Oral Health of Prisoners to Improve Overall Health and Well-Being. American Journal of Public Health: October 2005, Vol. 95, No. 10, pp. 1677-1678. doi: 10.2105/AJPH.2005.073924

57 Kuhn, C. (n.d.). Natural Medicine of Humor Adds Happiness to Your Life Right Away.natural-humor-medicine.com. Retrieved January 21, 2013, from http://www.natural-humor-medicine.com/

58 Strack, Martin, Stepper, 1988

59 Bulochova, V. (2011, January 27). The Smile Effect. suite101.com. Retrieved March 29, 2012, from http://veronika-bulochova.suite101.com/the-smile-effect-a339111

60 Ferreira-Schut, N. (2010, April 8). Does smiling lead to longevity and perceptions of attractiveness? suite101.com. Retrieved March 29, 2012, from http://nivea-ferreira-schut.suite101.com/live-longer-and-look-trustworthy-and-attractive-just-smile-a222542

61 Abel, E. L., & Kruger, M. L. (2010). Smile intensity in photographs predicts longevity.psychological science, 21(4), 542-544. doi:10.1177/0956797610363775

62 Certifiedhealthnut (2011, September 27). Troy Casey Longevity Secrets with 95 year old expert [Video File]. Retrieved from http://www.youtube.com/watch?v=oC0qRrT2EtE

63 Hay House UK (2011, May 12). David R. Hamilton explains how smiling is contagious [Video File]. Retrieved from http://www.youtube.com/watch?v=fHQBghevMLw&feature=related

64 SmilingChi (2010, July 4). Smiling and the Inner Smile [Video File]. Retrieved from http://www.youtube.com/watch?v=ML5uQAHQHVs&feature=related

65 Anandayoga (2011, January 25). Face Exercise 3 for Perfect Smile [Video File]. Retrieved from http://www.youtube.com/watch?v=r_0a63QQroE&feature= related

66 HealthyPeople.gov (n.d.). Oral Health Leading Health Indicators. Healthy People 2020 - Improving the Health of Americans. Retrieved January 20, 2013, from http://www.healthypeople.gov/2020/LHI/oralHealth.aspx

67 Ekman, P. (2004). In Emotions revealed: Recognizing faces and feelings to improve communication and emotional life (1st ed.). New York, N.Y: Henry Holt and Co.

68 Ekman, P. (2009). Telling lies: Clues to deceit in the marketplace, politics, and marriage. New York, NY: W.W. Norton.

69 Ereleases (2008, April 24). 'Size Does Matter ... and So Does Shape ... When It Comes to Teeth,' Says Cosmetic Dentist, Dr. Denise Fundora - Press Release. Press Release Distribution | Press Release Distribution Services. Retrieved December 20, 2012, from http://www.ereleases.com/pr/size-does-matter-and-so-does-shape-when-it-comes-to-teeth-says-cosmetic-dentist-dr-denise-fundora-12008

70 Goldstein, R. E. (2009). Change your smile: Discover how a new smile can transform your life (4th ed.). Hanover Park, IL: Quintessence Pub.

71 Fritsky, L. (2010, April 8). Get the best smile for your face. she knows health and wellness. Retrieved March 6, 2012, from http:// www.sheknows.com/health-and-wellness/articles/814593/get-the-best-smile-for-your-face-1

72 Huefner, N. (n.d.). Tooth Length. Huefner Sensational Smiles. Retrieved April 2, 2011, from http://cosmetic-dentistry-and-porcelain-veneers.com/smile-design/tooth-length-porcelain-veneers-porcelain-crowns/

73 Huefner, N. (n.d.). Tooth Length. Huefner Sensational Smiles. Retrieved April 2, 2011, from http://cosmetic-dentistry-and-porcelain-veneers.com/smile-design/tooth-length-porcelain-veneers-porcelain-crowns/

74 Pickthebrain15 Fascinating Facts About Smiling [Web log post]. Retrieved from http://Enter URLwww.pickthebrain.com/blog/15-fascinating-facts-about-smiling/

75 Fritsky, L. (2010, April 8). Get the best smile for your face. she knows health and wellness. Retrieved March 6, 2012, from http:// www.sheknows.com/health-and-wellness/articles/814593/get-the-best-smile-for-your-face-1

76   Rondon, N. (n.d.). Anatomy of a Smile. Consumer guide to dentistry. Retrieved March 3, 2011, from http:// www.yourdentistryguide.com/smile-anatomy

77   Rufenacht, C. R. (1990). In Fundamentals of esthetics (1st ed.). Chicago: Quintessence Pub. Co.

78   Rufenacht, C. R. (1990). In Fundamentals of esthetics (1st ed.). Chicago: Quintessence Pub. Co.

79   Goldstein, R. E. (2009). Change your smile: Discover how a new smile can transform your life (4th ed.). Hanover Park, IL: Quintessence Pub.

80   Rufenacht, C. R. (1990). In Fundamentals of esthetics (1st ed.). Chicago: Quintessence Pub. Co.

81   Strajni, L. (2002). Determination of placement of anterior teeth in removable dental prostheses.Med Pregl, 55(11-12), 490-492.

82   Rondon, N. (n.d.). Anatomy of a Smile. Consumer guide to dentistry. Retrieved March 3, 2011, from http:// www.yourdentistryguide.com/smile-anatomy

83   Rondon, N. (n.d.). Anatomy of a Smile. Consumer guide to dentistry. Retrieved March 3, 2011, from http:// www.yourdentistryguide.com/smile-anatomy

84   Pitstop (2010, November 10). Social Smile - an Interesting Comparison! Bukisa - Share Your Knowledge. Retrieved January 21, 2013, from http://www.bukisa.com/articles/392378_social-smile-an-interesting-comparison#ixzz1ICq9pXOm

85   Blewitt, P., & Broderick, P. C. (2006). In The Life Span - Human Development for Helping Professionals (3rd ed., p. 113).

86   Vooktv (2010, June 11). An Experiment by Joseph Campos: The Visual Cliff [Video File]. Retrieved from http://www.youtube.com/watch?v=p6cqNhHrMJA &tracker=False

87   Babylilafrog (2010, April 30). baby's first infant smiles (Day 64-69) [Video File]. Retrieved from http://www.youtube.com/watch?v=hp-V5xWVPfU

88   Ehow (2008, December 27). Child Care & Development : Baby Development Milestones [Video File]. Retrieved from http://www.youtube.com/watch?v=HNizU5Jbhuw

89   Drmdk (2008, March 8). Social Smile - Developmental Milestones [Video File]. Retrieved from http://www.youtube.com/watch?v=HzmWAi_5Q9o

90   Umassboston (2009, November 30). Still Face Experiment: Dr. Edward Tronick [Video File]. Retrieved from http://www.youtube.com/watch?v=apzXGEbZht0

91 Arredondo, D. E. (2009, March 4). Attunement and Why it Matters [Video File]. Retrieved from http://www.youtube.com/watch?v=URpuKgKt9kg&feature=related

92 Henson , S. T., Lindauer, S. J., Gardner, W. G., Shroff, B., Tufekci, E., & Best, A. M. (2011). Influence of dental esthetics on social perceptions of adolescents judged by peers.American Journal Orthod Dentofacial Orthop., 140(3), 389-95. doi:10.1016

93 Henson , S. T., Lindauer, S. J., Gardner, W. G., Shroff, B., Tufekci, E., & Best, A. M. (2011). Influence of dental esthetics on social perceptions of adolescents judged by peers.American Journal Orthod Dentofacial Orthop., 140(3), 389-95. doi:10.1016

94 Restored Church of God (RCG). (2003). Smile! Retrieved from http://rcg.org/youth/articles/0101-s.html

95 Relax Kids (2010, October 1). Self Esteem and Teens [Web log post]. Retrieved from blog.relaxkids.com/?p=2075

96 Nicholson, C. (n.d.). Smile. Inspirational Poems for Everyday Living. Retrieved February 8, 2012, from http://poetry.wholesomebalance.com/#smile

97 Lex2011 (n.d.). Smile | Teen Poem | Teen Ink. Teen Ink | A teen literary magazine and website. Retrieved September 8, 2012, from http://teenink.com/poetry/all/article/354514/Smile/

98 Beauty and Bedlam (n.d.). Importance of a Smile, Building Confidence in Children — Balancing Beauty and Bedlam. Balancing Beauty and Bedlam — One Frugal Mom's Attempt at Balancing it All. Retrieved August 6, 2012, from http://beautyandbedlam.com/importance-of-a-smile

99 Tung, A. W., & Kiyak, H. A. (1998). Psychological influences on the timing of orthodontic treatment. 113(1), 29-39.

100 Burke Qualtrough, E. J.A. J. (1994). Aesthetic inlays: composite or ceramic? British Dental Journal, 176(2), 53-60.

101 Kiyak, H. A. (2008). Does Orthodontic Treatment Affect Patients' Quality of Life? Journal of Dental Education, 72(8), 886-894.

102 American Dental Association (n.d.). Teen Teeth Article | Teenagers | Colgate® Oral Care Information Teenagers. Colgate. Retrieved March 25, 2012, from http://www.colgate.com/app/CP/US/EN/OC/Information/Articles/Oral-and-Dental-Health-at-Any-Age/Teenagers/Teen-Issues/article/Teen-Talk-Teen-Teeth.cvsp

103 Corter, C., Minde, K., Trehub, S., Boukydis, C., Celhoffer, L., & Marton, P. (1978). Mother-child relationships in premature nursery: an observational study. Pediatrics, 61(3), 373-377.

104 Clifford, M. M., & Walster, E. (1973). The effect of physical attractiveness on teacher expectations. Sociology of Education, 46(2), 248-258.

105 Willis, J., & Todorov, A. (2006). First impressions making up your mind after a 100-Ms exposure to a face. Psychological Science, 17(7), 592-598.

106 DentistryIQ (n.d.). A restored smile and renewed hope. DentistryIQ - Dental practice management, dental services & dental education for dentists. Retrieved February 25, 2012, from http://www.dentistryiq.com/articles/2012/01/a-restored-smile-and-renewed-hope.html

107 My Health Report (n.d.). Dental Decay Risk Assessment Calculator. My Health Report - Patient Report and Education Center. Retrieved June 14, 2012, from http://333.myhealthreport.info/rac/cosmetic-smile-self-analysis-calculator.php

108 Kinde, J. (n.d.). Smile Power--Increase Your Face Value. Humor Power. Retrieved May 21, 2012, from http://www.humorpower.com/smile_power.html

109 Bweuser (2009, November 9). Larry King Live SMIZE [Video File]. Retrieved from http://www.youtube.com/watch?v=LjXAnWnL9m0.

www.ingramcontent.com/pod-product-compliance
Lightning Source LLC
Chambersburg PA
CBHW030428290526
45786CB00001B/189